PRAISE FOR THE
UNCOMMON JUNIOR HIGH GROUP STUDIES

The best junior high/middle school curriculum to come out in years.

Jim Burns, Ph.D.
President, HomeWord

A landmark resource for years to come.

Chapman R. Clark, Ph.D.
Associate Professor of Youth and Family Ministry
Fuller Theological Seminary

The *Uncommon* Junior High curriculum is truly "cross-cultural." Built on the solid foundation of an understanding of junior-highers' unique developmental needs and rapidly changing culture, it affords teachers and youth workers the opportunity to communicate God's unchanging Word to kids growing up in a world that increasingly muffles and muddles the truth.

Walt Mueller
President, Center for Parent/Youth Understanding
Author of *Understanding Today's Youth Culture*

The creators and writers of this curriculum know and love young teens, and that's what sets good junior high curriculum apart from the mediocre stuff!

Mark Oestreicher
President, Youth Specialties

This is serious curriculum for junior-highers! Not only does it take the great themes of the Christian faith seriously, but it takes junior-highers seriously as well.

Wayne Rice
Founder and Director, Understanding Your Teenager Seminars

It fleshes out . . . two absolute essentials for great curriculum: biblical depth and active learning.

Duffy Robbins
Associate Professor, Department of Youth Ministry
Eastern College

uncommon
be extraordinary

PARENTS & FAMILY

KARA POWELL
General Editor

Published by Gospel Light
Ventura, California, U.S.A.
www.gospellight.com
Printed in the U.S.A.

All Scripture quotations are taken from the *Holy Bible, New International Version*®.
Copyright © 1973, 1978, 1984 by International Bible Society.
Used by permission of Zondervan Publishing House. All rights reserved.

© 2000, 2010 Gospel Light.
All rights reserved.

Unit 1, "Parents and Family," previously published as Pulse #9: *Home and Family*
in the *Life Issues* track. Unit 2, "Family and Friends," never before published.

Contributing writers: Tim Baker; Kara Powell, Ph.D.; Natalie Chenault and Siv Ricketts.

Library of Congress Cataloging-in-Publication Data
Uncommon jr. high group study : parents & family / Kara Powell, general editor.
p. cm.
ISBN 978-0-8307-5099-3 (trade paper)
1. Families—Religious aspects—Christianity—Study and teaching. 2. Church work
with children. 3. Junior high school students—Religious life—Study and teaching.
I. Powell, Kara. II. Title: Uncommon junior high group study.
BT707.7.U53 2010
268'.433—dc22
2010000942

Rights for publishing this book outside the U.S.A. or in non-English languages are
administered by Gospel Light Worldwide, an international not-for-profit ministry.
For additional information, please visit www.glww.org, email info@glww.org, or write
to Gospel Light Worldwide, 1957 Eastman Avenue, Ventura, CA 93003, U.S.A.

Contents

How to Use the *Uncommon* Junior High Group Studies

Each *Uncommon* junior high group study contains 12 sessions, which are divided into 2 stand-alone units of 6 sessions each. You may choose to teach all 12 sessions consecutively, or to use just one unit, or to present each session separately. You know your group, so do what works best for you and your students.

This is your leader's guidebook for teaching your group. Electronic files (in PDF format) for each session's student handouts are available online at www.gospellight.com/uncommon_jh_parents_and_family.zip. The handouts include the "Reflect" section of each study, formatted for easy printing, in addition to any student worksheets for the session. You may print as many copies as you need for your group.

Each individual session begins with a brief overview of the "big idea" of the lesson, the aims of the session, the primary Bible verse and additional verses that tie in to the topic being discussed. Each of the 12 sessions is geared to be 45 to 90 minutes in length and is comprised of two options that you can choose from, based on the type of group that you have. Option 1 tends to be a more active learning experience, while Option 2 tends to be a more discussion-oriented exercise.

The sections in each session are as follows:

Starter

Young people will stay in your youth group longer if they feel comfortable and make friends. This first section helps students get to know each other better and focus on the theme of the lesson in a fun and engaging way.

Message

The Message section enables students to look up to God by relating the words of Scripture to the session topic.

Dig

Unfortunately, many young people are biblically illiterate. In this section, students look inward and discover how God's Word connects with their own world.

Apply

Young people need the opportunity to think through the issues at hand. The apply section leads students out into their world with specific challenges to apply at school, at home and with their friends.

Reflect

This concluding section of the study allows students to reflect on the material presented in the session. You can print these pages from the PDF found at www.gospellight.com/uncommon_jh_parents_and_family.zip and give them to your students as a handout for them to work on throughout the week.

Want More Options?

An additional option for each section, along with accompanying worksheets, is available in PDF format at www.gospellight.com/uncommon_jh_parents_and_family.zip.

UNIT I
Parents & Family

We can catch glimpses of how families have changed over the last few decades by peering into the cultural mirror provided to us by television families. Ward and June Cleaver focused their attention almost exclusively on their sons, concerned with how they could use everything that happened to Wally and "the Beaver" to teach important life lessons. Cliff and Claire Huxtable, while still focusing much of their time on their five children, had their own careers, their own interests and even their own sex life. (Imagine that!) Homer and Marge Simpson maintain two distinct relationships with their very independent children: Homer plays the self-absorbed, lazy father and Marge the well-meaning yet fairly helpless mother. What they share is a distant role in the lives of their autonomous, preadolescent children.

Your junior-highers' families may be somewhat different from the one that raised you. What we see in television families, and probably what you see in the families of your junior-highers, confirms that many parents are absorbed with their own needs and interests. Decisions about family matters are often based on what is best or easiest for the parents, with children left either emotionally neglected or forced to grow up too fast. Young adolescents lack the skills to take care of themselves, yet their well-meaning but often busy and preoccupied parents aren't around enough to do it for them.

As a result, many junior-highers are confused about what their family *is*, *what it is supposed to be* and *who they are supposed to be* in it. Thankfully, God's Word has a lot to say on the matter. This study is committed to helping students understand what God's written and incarnated Word has to say about the family and their place in it, through three strategies.

1. *Reality-based stories.* Forty percent of the students in your youth ministry will go to sleep tonight in a home without their father. That's their reality. This book doesn't hide from unfortunate truths like that, but it places a biblical spotlight on them and helps students

navigate through the stormy waters of their parents' divorce, step-parent dynamics and sibling rivalry.

2. *Easy-to-grasp principles.* The youth workers involved in this study have spent years with junior-highers (and sometimes their own children!) getting to know not just what they feel but how they think. As a result, they have packed this book full of concrete examples, simple principles and tangible application steps that will likely reach even your most confused sixth grader.

3. *A model of what should be.* The danger in focusing only on students' reality is that it omits God's ideal. This study tries to walk the fine line of identifying and empathizing with what students are experiencing, while giving them a vision for what might be better and what they might want to do when—*gasp, shudder*—they have kids of their own.

Kara Powell
Executive Director of the Fuller Youth Institute
Assistant Professor of Youth, Family and Culture
Fuller Theological Seminary

MAKING IT EASY

THE BIG IDEA

Students can make their parents' lives a lot easier.

SESSION AIMS

In this session you will guide students to (1) understand the ability they have to help or hinder their parents; (2) discover tangible ways they can help and encourage their parents; and (3) commit to make their parents' lives easier this week.

THE BIGGEST VERSE

"Children, obey your parents in the Lord, for this is right. 'Honor your father and mother'—which is the first commandment with a promise—'that it may go well with you and that you may enjoy long life on the earth'" (Ephesians 6:1-3).

OTHER IMPORTANT VERSES

Genesis 9:18-29; Luke 9:57-62; Ephesians 4:29

Note: Additional options and worksheets in 8$^1/_2$" x 11" format for this session are available for download at **www.gospellight.com/uncommon_jh_parents_and_family.zip**.

STARTER

Option 1: Adult Stress Check. For this option, you need copies of "Adult Stress Check" (found on the next page) and pens or pencils.

Greet students and explain that you're diving into a new series about families, and then briefly discuss the following:

- If you were to describe what this last week has been like for your parents, what words would you use?
- Why those words?
- How about during the last month?
- Do you think your parents have an easier or harder life than you do?

Explain that the group is now going to do an activity to help them think about their parents' lives. Distribute "Adult Stress Check" and pens or pencils and ask students to circle any stressful situations that their parents have experienced recently. After they've completed the handouts, take a poll to determine which situations parents have experienced the most and which they've experienced the least. Then discuss the following:

- What does this tell you about your parents' lives?
- Are you someone who adds stress to your parents' lives or reduces it?
- What do you do that causes your parents the most stress?
- What do you do that helps them the most?

Explain that today the group is going to spend some time discussing how we can help our parents—and why we should.

Option 2: Keepers of the Wrap. For this option, you need one medium-sized box for every 10 students, wrapping paper and transparent tape. Ahead of time, wrap each box with wrapping paper. (*Note:* This activity will be rough on the boxes, so consider wrapping them twice!)

Greet the students, and then divide them into groups of 10 and ask everyone to remove their shoes. Designate half of each group as the "Unwrappers" and the other half as the "Keepers of the Wrap." The Unwrappers will try to unwrap a gift using their feet, while the Keepers of the Wrap will use their feet to stop the Unwrappers.

While teams work out their strategies, place the gift boxes in the center of the room. (*Note:* For a less chaotic option, have groups sit in chairs in a circle

ADULT STRESS CHECK

Put a checkmark by every stressful situation that your parents have experienced in the last 6 to 12 months.

- ☑ Household repairs
- ☑ Job instability or work pressure
- ☐ Conflict with their parents
- ☐ Conflict with their siblings
- ☐ Conflict with you
- ☑ Conflict with your siblings
- ☐ Personal health problems
- ☑ Health problems of a loved one
- ☐ The death of a loved one
- ☐ Dealing with ex-spouse or with blended families

- ☑ Busy schedule
- ☑ Financial struggles
- ☐ Taking care of their parents
- ☐ Worrying about their siblings
- ☑ Worrying about you
- ☑ Worrying about your siblings
- ☐ Fatigue
- ☐ Divorce or separation
- ☐ Fear of not being good parents
- ☑ Dealing with their own weaknesses and sin

---

and place the boxes in the center of each group's circle.) Designate a box for each set of Unwrappers and Keepers of the Wrap, and then give the signal to begin the game. You might have to remind them again to use only their feet.

After a few minutes, stop the game and remove the boxes from the teams' reach. When the game is over, discuss the following:

- In this game, the Unwrappers worked together to unwrap the boxes and the Keepers of the Wrap worked together to stop them. Unwrappers, how did you help each other? Keepers, how did you help each other?

- In your daily life, what keeps you from helping others? *Too much work, too busy, and so forth.*

- What are the benefits of helping others? *Helps the other person feel good, helps me feel good, showing God's love and kindness, and so on.*

Explain that today you're going to start a new series about our families. When it comes to our parents, even the simplest things we do can help them or make their lives a lot more difficult.

MESSAGE

Option 1: Bible Charades. For this option, you will need several Bibles and candy prizes.

Explain to the group that while it's easy to think that the people in the Bible never struggled with their relationships with their parents, the truth is that teens and parents have always struggled with getting along! Today we're going to check out one situation where three brothers had different reactions to their father's embarrassing situation.

Divide students into groups of two to four and distribute a Bible to each group. Whisper a different verse from Genesis 9:18-29 to each group; then an-

Youth Leader Tip

Make sure to stress that when you say "parents," you mean any adult who is helping to raise the teen. For many students, that will include stepparents, parents who live in different houses, aunts, uncles, foster parents and grandparents.

nounce that groups have five minutes to come up with a way to portray what is happening in their assigned verses *without speaking*. (It's okay if you don't have enough students to cover all the verses.) *Everyone* in each group must be involved, so some groups might have to get creative with scenery and props (one student can be a rock and two students can pose as the cave, and so on).

In random order, have each group act out its assigned verse while the other students use their Bibles to try to figure out which verse the group is acting out. Whoever yells out the correct verse first earns 500 points for his or her team. At the end of the verses, award the candy to the team with the most points and ask the winning team to read Genesis 9:18-29 aloud.

Explain that Ham had the chance to do the right thing, but he didn't. He avoided helping his father and went outside to tell his brothers. You can almost imagine how it sounded when Ham told his brothers about their dad being naked. Ham's brothers didn't react the way he did, though. After hearing what happened to their father, they helped him in the most discreet way they knew how: They walked backward and laid a blanket, which they had been carrying over their shoulders, over Noah. And all without ever seeing his nakedness! That shows how determined they were to help their dad and not to embarrass or disrespect him.[1]

Option 2: Shame or Respect? For this option, you need several Bibles, copies of "Shame or Respect?" (found on the next page) and masking or transparent tape. Ahead of time, cut apart the questions on the handout, creating several sets of each question.

Distribute Bibles and read Genesis 9:18-29. Tape one of the questions from "Shame or Respect?" to each student's back, and then ask students to find partners. Each partner should silently read the question on his or her partner's back, and then answer the question aloud—*without sharing the question*. When students in each pair have answered their partner's questions, they are to find new partners and repeat the process.

Continue for a few minutes, and then give the signal to stop. Invite several students to guess the question on their back. Allow for a few responses, and then invite everyone to remove and read the question taped to their back. Ask students who have Question 1 to share some of the answers others gave them. Repeat this for the rest of the questions.

Remind the group of the passage you read before the game—about Noah having too much to drink and passing out in an embarrassing position. End of story, right? Wrong. The real story began when Ham had the opportunity to

Shame or RESPECT?

QUESTION 1:

What Did Ham do that was wrong?

QUESTION 2:

How did Shem and Japheth help their dad?

QUESTION 3:

What motivated Shem and Japheth to cover their dad?

QUESTION 4:

Which brother do you relate to the most?

QUESTION 5:

What would you have done?

help his dad but instead chose to disrespect his father by bringing Noah's nakedness to the attention of Shem and Japheth. Shem and Japheth reacted to
the situation in a different way. They chose to help their dad, and the way they
did it was pretty tricky: They walked backward with a blanket on their shoulders
and laid it over Noah. They took great pains to do this and never once saw
Noah's nakedness! That shows how determined they were to help their dad and
not to embarrass or disrespect him.

DIG

Option 1: Anointed with Oil. For this option, you need a whiteboard, a dry-
erase marker, copies of "Anointed with Oil" (found on the next two pages) and
a few oil cans. Ahead of time, give the skit to several students so they can practice their parts.[2]

As students come forward to present the skit, explain that sometimes it can
be difficult to think up ways to help our parents. As they watch this skit, have
them think of ways that they might help their parents. After the performance,
applaud the actors; then read Ephesians 4:29 and 6:1-3. Discuss:

- Who do you encourage more—your parents or your friends?
- Who do you honor more—your parents or your friends?
- Why do you think that is?

Explain that these passages give us great guidelines for how we're supposed to help our parents. We're supposed to obey them, but we're also supposed to treat them like we would anyone else—with encouragement and
support. Just like we saw here, it might be hard at first, but once we get used
to doing it and do it more regularly, our entire family will benefit.

Ask students to describe something tough that their parents are going
through, and then see if the rest of the group can come up with ways to encourage, honor and obey their parents in the midst of what they are experiencing. (*Caution:* Don't let this become a gossip or griping session. Encourage
students to speak in generalities: "My dad is worried about trouble at work" or
"My mom is tired because she takes care of my grandma.") Write these on the
whiteboard and then discuss:

- What do these problems have in common? *They cause stress, worry, fatigue, and so on.*

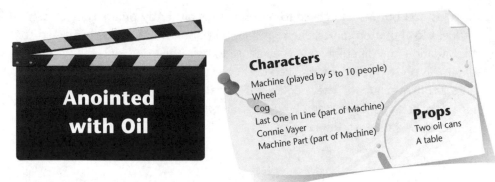

Anointed with Oil

Characters
Machine (played by 5 to 10 people)
Wheel
Cog
Last One in Line (part of Machine)
Connie Vayer
Machine Part (part of Machine)

Props
Two oil cans
A table

A line of 5 to 10 skit players (the Machine) are onstage acting out the movements of a machine: One player makes a machinelike movement; another player builds a movement onto the Machine that reacts to the first movement, and so on. Each plays a part in the Machine—hissing, pinging and whirring toward some productive end. But there are some key parts missing. The Machine chugs on a few moments, though it's perfectly clear the work is hindered. The Machine parts frown and look around, wondering what's happening. The noises become more and more discordant and halting. Cog and Wheel enter, moving stiffly and mechanically, like rusted tin men.

Machine: (*Separate people taking separate lines*) Hey, where you guys been?! Nothing's getting done over here! We need you! Snap to! Fall in! Line up!

Wheel: (*Waving to Machine while talking to Cog out of the side of his mouth*) Hey, Cog! Looks like we're in hot water again.

Cog: Looks like it, Wheel. I'm movin' a little slow today. You?

Wheel: You don't know the half of it.

Cog and Wheel do limber-up exercises.

Cog: Man, I need to spend more time working out. I'm draggin'.

Wheel: No kidding! My joints are all . . .

Machine: (*together*) Come on! (*separately*) You're holdin' up progress! We gotta move ahead! Time's wasting! Hurry up! Move it!

Cog: Look, we need to be in shape or we're not going to get anywhere.

Wheel: No kidding.

Cog and Wheel produce oil cans and lubricate their joints. They shake the cans and look inside.

Wheel: Hey, I didn't bring a whole lot of oil today. I think I've got just enough left for another lube.

Cog: Same here. Hey, you guys bring any extra oil in case we . . .

Machine: (*together*) No! (*separately*) Getting oil's your job! I've only got enough for me! I didn't bring any extra! I oil up at home! (*together*) Now get in line!

Cog and Wheel shrug and get in line. The Machine chugs along in harmony. In mime, the Machine parts pass something invisible down the line. Last One in Line turns, like a pair of robotic arms, and drops the "product" on the floor, making the sound of a crash. The passing and crashing is repeated several times.

Machine: (*With separate people taking separate lines*) Hey, what's going on down there?! What's the crashing noise? What's breakin' down? We're doin' our part over here!

Last One in Line: I can't help it, you Bozos! Somebody's missin'!

Cog: It's Connie. Connie Vayer. She's not in her place at the end. We can't finish anything without her.

As they speak, Connie Vayer walks in. She grinds forward like a toy whose batteries are running low and then stops, moves a little forward and then stops. Finally, near center she halts and tips forward.

Wheel: Look, there she is.

Connie: (weakly, stiff-jawed) Heeelp meee. (*The Machine keeps chugging away.*)

Machine: She looks terrible. What's her problem? A couple of quarts low, looks like to me. She shoulda took care of herself at home. Nope, I don't have anything for her.

Connie: Heeelp meee.

Cog: We gotta help her, Wheel, or nothin'll get done.

Wheel: Both of us don't have any extra oil. I've just got what I need in case I start to lose steam.

Cog: How about it, everybody? Let's lend her some oil . . .

Machine: (*together*) No! There's only enough for me!

Connie: (*barely understandable*) Oiiiil caaan.

Cog: How 'bout it, Wheel?

Wheel: I can't afford to break down.

Cog: Neither can I. But if you give her a little and I give her a little, we'll both pull this off. And we'll have enough for the both of us. Got it?

Wheel thinks a bit and then nods. They step out. Immediately the Machine becomes discordant. They oil Connie's joints. She stands, moves her limbs and then starts to walk. She tries to talk.

Wheel: What's she sayin'?

Cog: I think she said, "My mouth." She wants us to oil her jaw.

Wheel: Think we should leave that part rusty?

Cog: (*smacking him*) Oil it! (*They oil each side of her jaw.*)

Connie: Thanks, you sweet things, you! Wow, what a relief. Now I can move anywhere I want. Incredible! I just can't believe you two would sacrifice some of your . . .

Machine: Come on!

Wheel: (*to Cog*) Told ya.

They all jump back in line. The Machine works in harmony again. Connie is there to pick up the imaginary products and carry them to the table, where she is now stacking them up. For a moment, we listen to the well-oiled machinery.

Machine: That's better! Now we're cookin' with gas! Er, with oil! What a sound! Purrin' like a cat!

One of the Machine parts suddenly halts a little.

Machine Part: Hey, just felt a little stiffness. In my elbows, I think. Can anybody spare a little oil? I ran out this morning. (*Silence. Cog and Wheel look at each other.*)

Machine: (*separately*) I think so. Sure, I got a little extra in my back pocket. Gotcha, dude, fix ya right up. No worries around here.

Machine Part: Thanks.

Cog and Wheel look at each other and smile. The Machine continues purring on.

- What kind of attitude do we need to have in order to help our parents?
  A loving, serving, Christlike attitude.

- How can we develop this kind of attitude? *You might want to point out here that the more you do something, the more natural it seems. The more we help our parents, the more it becomes a habit for us, and the easier it will be. You could compare it to practicing a skill such as drawing, throwing a ball or playing a musical instrument.*

Option 2: Ways You Can Help. For this option, you will need paper and pens or pencils.

Explain that Noah was caught in an embarrassing situation and two of his sons did the right thing and helped him. Most of us probably haven't had to help our parents in such an extreme way, but chances are we've all seen our parents encounter a problem—simple or difficult—that they've needed help with. Right now, we're going to explore some of the things that parents might need help with.

Divide students into groups of four and give each group a sheet of paper and a pen or pencil. Ask groups to choose one real-life situation they've faced when their parents have needed help and write the situation at the *top* of the paper.

Allow a few moments for brainstorming, and then have groups exchange papers. Instruct each group to write at the *bottom* of the new page one suggestion that a junior-higher could do to help their parents in that situation. When groups are finished writing, papers should be passed off to the next group and new suggestions should be written. Ideas can't be used more than once—each group must come up with a new idea. Repeat the exchanges several times, and then ask groups to return the papers to the original groups. Give them time to read the responses to their original situations, and ask each group to share its original situation as well as the best suggestion given by another group.

APPLY

Option 1: Five for Five. For this option, you need one nickel for every student.

Explain that sometimes it's good to start with small steps when we're trying to change something. That means starting out small and gradually making bigger changes.

Offer a nickel to every student who is willing to spend at least five minutes every day for the next week helping out his or her parents. Brainstorm ways to help out, like emptying the dishwasher, carrying in the groceries, clearing the table after dinner or vacuuming the family room. Stress that only students who are *really* willing to follow through with their commitment to help out should raise their hands to receive a nickel, and ask them to keep their nickels where they can see them as a reminder to spend their time helping out.

Close in prayer, asking God to show each student how to be a blessing to his or her parents in the coming week.

Option 2: Pop What You Will Stop. For this option, you will need one large balloon for each student, felt-tip pens, a jumbo-sized garbage bag (or two) and a needle.

Explain that all of us have a choice about whether we're going to help our parents or not. But it's hard to think about how we can make their lives easier until we've examined how we make their lives difficult.

Distribute the balloons and felt-tip pens, and then instruct each student to inflate their balloon. Invite them to use a pen to write a few words on their balloon that describe some ways they were *unhelpful* to their parents in the past week. When they've finished, invite them to share what they've written.

Once everyone has had a chance to share, invite students to come forward who would like to commit to helping their parents. Have them place their balloons in the garbage bag and share aloud one *positive* thing they will do for their parents this week, replacing the negative things they have done in the past. When all are through placing their balloons in the bag, use the needle to pop all of them as a symbol of the end of students' old, unhelpful ways.

Spend time praying, thanking God for students' families and asking Him to help students keep their commitments.

Youth Leader Tip

Remember next week to ask students if they kept their commitments to help their parents. Also make sure to allow time for them to share what they did and how their parents responded.

REFLECT

The following short devotions are for the students to reflect on and answer during the week. You can make a copy of these pages and distribute to your class or print out from the PDF available online at **www.gospellight.com/uncommon_jh_parents_and_family.zip**.

1—NOTE FROM MOM

Hey you! Go get filled up on Colossians 3:20 right now!

Imagine that you come home from school and see a note from your mom on the door of the refrigerator. The note says: "Hi! Hope you had a good day at school! Please take out the trash, feed the dog and do your homework. Don't watch too much TV! I'll be home around 6:00 P.M." What do you do?

❑ Read the note, grab the chips and lay on the couch watching TV until your mom comes home.
❑ Read the note and do everything except take out the trash. You'll just tell your mom you forgot, or make your little brother do it later.
❑ Ignore the note (because you know if you read it, you'll have to work) and head to your friend's house to play video games.
❑ Read the note and do everything on it as fast as you can so that you can go outside and ride your skateboard.
❑ Read the note, take out the trash and feed the dog; but forget about doing your homework because your mom won't know the difference.

When your mom or dad asks you to do something, do you do it? Or do you make excuses or try to get out of doing what they ask?

_____

_____

_____

_____

Do you ever just flat-out ignore your parents when they ask you to do something? How do you think that makes them feel?

_____

_____

_____

_____

2—SERVING AT HOME

Read Ephesians 6:2-3 to find out about your reward.

Danny loved to go on mission trips with his junior high group. It made him feel really good when he served because he knew God wanted him to—and because most of the time it was a lot of fun.

Danny's dad really encouraged him to volunteer and be a servant. Danny was always very willing to do anything for his church. At home, however, it was another story. Danny didn't want to do anything. Whenever his dad asked him to do anything—clean the kitchen, vacuum or pick up his room—Danny would roll his eyes and grumble and treat his dad like he was a jerk for even asking.

God calls us to be servants to everybody—our friends, our enemies and (gulp) even our parents! It's easy to forget that when we come home and our parents ask us to do something, we need to do it! Be a servant to everyone you meet today—including your parents!

3—OBEDIENCE AND RESPECT

Go read Proverbs 13:1 and get smart!

Imagine that you and some of your friends have decided it would be fun to climb up on the roof of your house—and your mom catches you. She gets really mad and makes everyone come down. What kind of a reaction do you think you might have in front of your friends?

- ❑ "My mom is *so* dumb. She doesn't want me to have *any* fun. We'll just climb up there when she isn't around."
- ❑ "I don't care if my mom thinks walking around on the roof is stupid and dangerous. I'm gonna do it anyway."
- ❑ "Maybe my mom is right. She probably knows a lot of things I don't and I know that she cares about me enough to keep me safe, so maybe I should listen to her."

How do you react when your mom or dad tells you *not* to do something? Do you roll your eyes and do it anyway?

_____

_____

_____

_____

Do you tell yourself how dumb and out of touch your parents are? Or do you trust that they know what is best for you and obey what they say?

_____

_____

_____

_____

How do you think God wants you to react to your parents? Ask Him to help you be quick to obey your parents today, no matter how tough it is.

_____

_____

_____

_____

4—DAD KNOWS BEST

Find Ephesians 6:1. You won't be sorry!

Angie was so excited that she'd been invited to the party at Emily's house. Emily's parents were out of town and her older brother was left in charge of the house—and her brother was *so* cool that he was letting Emily throw a party! Angie couldn't wait to get there and hang out with all the popular kids, especially since she had spent all week planning what to wear.

The night of the party, Angie's dad came into her room and told her, "I know you really want to go to this party at Emily's, but I just found out that her parents won't be there and I don't want you to go."

Angie started crying. "But, Dad, Emily's so popular! If I don't show up tonight, she'll never want to hang out with me again and neither will any of the other cool kids! It's just not *fair*!"

Sometimes, obeying your parents can be really, really, *really* hard. It can mean doing chores you hate or not going where you want to go. God put your parents into your life for a reason, though, and you need to ask Him to help you obey and treat them the way He wants you to.

What are two things you can do this week to obey your parents?

_____

_____

_____

_____

AVAILABLE ADVICE

THE BIG IDEA

Your family is a place you can go to for advice.

SESSION AIMS

In this session you will guide students to (1) understand the resources available to them through their parents; (2) feel empowered to overcome obstacles that keep them from seeking the advice of their parents or other family members; and (3) commit to asking their families for advice in one area of their lives.

THE BIGGEST VERSE

"Listen to advice and accept instruction, and in the end you will be wise" (Proverbs 19:20).

OTHER IMPORTANT VERSES

Exodus 18:1-27; Proverbs 1:5; 12:15; Philippians 4:6

Note: Additional options and worksheets in 8¹/₂" x 11" format for this session are available for download at **www.gospellight.com/uncommon_jh_parents_and_family.zip**.

STARTER

Option 1: Bit of Advice. For this option, you need paper and pens or pencils.

Welcome students and divide them into groups of four. Explain that each group is going to be given a scenario and students are to decide what advice their parents might have for that situation. Distribute paper and pens or pencils, and explain that groups are to respond to their scenarios by writing only *the first three words* of advice that might be given by their parents. Then they are to pass their papers to another group, who will build on the advice by adding another three words before passing the paper on. The goal is to keep passing the papers until the advice is finished, and the result should be some pretty interesting—and sometimes hilarious—responses. Assign each group one of the following scenarios:

- Mom and Dad, I'm concerned about my grades.
- Mom and Dad, I've got a friend who's going to run away.
- Mom and Dad, I don't have any friends.
- Mom and Dad, I miss spending time with you.
- Mom and Dad, I think the most popular kid at school hates me.

After a few minutes, signal to stop passing the papers and have each group read the advice on their papers; then discuss the following:

- Did any of these pieces of advice resemble what your parents have said to you in the past?
- How are they different?
- On a scale of 1 to 10, with 10 being really valuable and 1 being totally worthless, what ranking would you give the advice you usually receive from your parents?
- How does your ranking make you feel?

Explain that asking family members for advice—or even for their opinion—isn't always the easiest thing to do. Why? Because we're often afraid that they won't understand us or they're going to give us bad advice—or, worse yet, we're going to have to listen to a lecture. Today, we're going to talk about how we can learn the most from the family members God has put into our lives.

Option 2: Net Advice. For this option, you need copies of "Net Advice" (found on the next page) and pens or pencils.

NET ADVICE

Read the following conversation below between your friends Visualgirl, #1Hockeyfan, Hastapasta and SK8ERDUDE. Where indicated, respond to your friends' statements about their family and give them some advice on how to handle the situation.

Visualgirl: Well, I'm having a good day. How's the rest of the crew today? ☺

#1Hockeyfan: Good.

Hastapasta: All systems go!

SK8ERDUDE: I've had better days. My parents have been fighting all week. Today, they started yelling in the kitchen and kept yelling all the way to the car.

[You]: _____

_____

#1Hockeyfan: All I know is that if my parents did that, I'd need a serious stack of drugs. That's the only way I could get through something like that.

Visualgirl: You mean you'd just skip school and do drugs? ☹ Not me, I'd go after my parents with something like a baseball bat.

[You]: _____

_____

Hastapasta: You know, my parents began yelling at each other once, and I threw a big tantrum and went to my room. They didn't stop yelling, and I felt stupid.

SK8ERDUDE: I really need advice on this. I want my parents to get along, and I don't want to do something (no offense) stupid like throw a tantrum or take chemicals.

[You]: _____

_____

Welcome students, divide them into groups of three, and then explain that today you are going to look at the issue of how they can get advice from their family. But before you do that, you need to talk about what advice really is. Distribute "Net Advice" and pens or pencils and allow time for groups to complete the handout. Let them know that their advice should be constructive without being too bossy. When everyone is done, invite groups to share their responses, and then discuss the following:

- What does it mean to give advice? *To give someone an opinion on what he or she should do in a particular situation.*
- When do you usually want advice? *When you're unsure about something or someone.*
- Are there times when you don't want someone's advice? *Sometimes it's hard to accept advice when you don't want to recognize that you are on the wrong path.*
- What kind of attitude do you need to have in order to receive advice? *An attitude of appreciation and acceptance—even if you don't end up following the advice.*
- What part does a family play in getting/giving advice? *Our families love us and their advice usually comes from concern for us.*
- When have you gone to your family for advice recently?

Explain that advice is an interesting thing; some of us like asking for it and others like giving it. Today we're going to check out what God's Word has to say about learning as much as we can from the people He's put in our lives to teach us—our families.

MESSAGE

Option 1: Give It to Moses! For this option, you need several Bibles and copies of "Give It to Moses!" (found on the next page).

Divide students into groups of four, distribute Bibles, and then explain that today they are going to take a look at a passage that tells about a time when Moses received advice from his father-in-law—advice that proved valuable to Moses.

Instruct groups to read Exodus 18:1-16, then distribute "Give It to Moses!" and set up the following scenario: "Imagine that you're there with Jethro and Moses. Jethro sees that Moses needs help, and he's about to give him some advice—but before he has the chance, you jump in with *your* advice."

GIVE IT TO MOSES

Moses needs your advice. Select one of the following topics and give it to him!

TOPIC ONE

Moses spends his entire day, from morning to night, judging disputes between people.

TOPIC TWO

Moses is doing all of the work alone.

TOPIC THREE

Moses makes all the decisions, from the littlest conflicts to the biggest disputes.

Explain that groups can give Moses advice on any one of the three topics on their handouts and that they are going to perform an impromptu role-play with one student acting as Moses and the other as Jethro. Allow time for groups to decide which topic to use, and then have them perform their role-plays. When they've finished, discuss the following:

- If you were Moses, what advice would you have found most helpful?
- What is the significance of Moses listening to and accepting his father-in-law's advice? *Moses was able to lead his people in a different way—he was able to delegate responsibility and authority to others, which was a more effective method of leadership.*
- If you were Moses and needed advice, would you have asked your father-in-law?

Explain that this shows Moses' willingness to listen to what his wife's father had to say. Read Exodus 18:17-27, and then read the following questions one at a time, allowing one or two minutes between each question for discussion within the small groups:

- If you were Moses, how might you have felt about your father-in-law's giving you advice?
- Do you agree with what Jethro said to Moses?
- Why do you think Moses did what his father-in-law said to do?

Explain to the group that the advice Jethro gave to Moses helped him lead the Israelites more effectively. Just as Jethro had good advice for Moses, our families often have solid advice for us as well—but we have to be willing to listen to what they have to say, and we have to be willing to act on what we hear.[1]

Youth Leader Tip

Be sure to make two important points clear to students: (1) Moses was supposed to remain God's representative to the Israelites, and (2) Moses' selection of the delegates was to be undertaken with great care.

Option 2: Who Do You Ask? For this option, you need several Bibles, paper and pens or pencils.

Begin by pointing out that we've all had times when we've needed to ask our family members for advice. Distribute paper and pens or pencils and instruct students to write the names of family members with whom they have regular contact. They don't need to live with the students, but they need to be people that students talk to, visit with or write to at least once a month.

After students have made their lists, ask them to circle the names of three family members that they would be most likely to go to if they needed advice about a conflict with a friend at school. Ask the group what it is about these three people that would make them want to go to them for advice. (Possible answers could include: They've given good advice in the past; they're followers of Jesus; they're easy to talk to; and so forth.)

Explain that oftentimes, the best place to go for advice is to our families. When Moses faced a difficult situation and needed some advice, he listened to one of his wise family members. Distribute Bibles and ask for several volunteers to read Exodus 18:1-27, taking turns every three verses or so, and then discuss the following:

- If you were Moses, how might you have felt about your father-in-law's giving you advice?
- Do you agree with what Jethro said to Moses?
- Why do you think Moses did what his father-in-law said he should do?
- If Moses had disagreed with Jethro's advice, what should he have done? *He should have shown respect and appreciation to him for his concern.*

Explain that it was important that Moses listened to his father-in-law and did what he advised—and it turned out that Jethro's advice really helped Moses. In the same way, it might not always be easy for us to accept advice, but we can get a lot of help from the advice our family members give us.

DIG

Option 1: When I Need Advice. For this option, you need several Bibles, copies of "When I Need Advice" (found on the next page) and pens or pencils.

Explain to the group that Jethro wasn't related to Moses by blood; they were related by marriage. Ask them to think about that for a moment. When people truly have your best interests in mind, their advice comes from caring

when i need advice

Hey! You've got some things in your life that you need advice about, right? How likely are you to ask for advice from someone in your family? List 10 things you need advice on, in the order of how likely you'd be to approach your family for advice on them.

I'd *definitely* go to my family for advice on:

   1. _____

   2. _____

   3. _____

   4. _____

   5. _____

I'd *consider* going to my family for advice on:

   6. _____

   7. _____

   8. _____

   9. _____

There's *no way* I would go to my family for advice on:

   10. _____

about you—how they are related to you doesn't matter. After all, sometimes we are related to people by blood, sometimes by marriage and sometimes by circumstances that have simply placed us within a family!

Distribute "When I Need Advice" and pens or pencils. Instruct students to list how likely they would be to ask their families for advice on particular topics. Encourage them to work individually, considering the dynamic in their own family.

Allow three minutes or so, then invite students to share with three other students what they've written. Allow several minutes for sharing, and then invite volunteers to share their lists with the rest of the group. Ask students to each choose one thing from their lists, and explain how they might go about asking for advice about that topic. Discuss the following:

- What would you *never* ask family members for advice about?
- Does everyone have to ask his or her family for advice?

Read Proverbs 1:5; 12:15 and 19:20, and then discuss the following:

- What do these passages say about asking for advice? *It's wise to seek advice and to listen when it's given.*
- What might happen when we don't ask the advice of our family? *We can miss out on learning something that might be really important.*
- Are we doomed? *Not unless we refuse to listen to the advice that we are offered by those who care about us!*

Explain that while it's one thing to read about Moses getting advice from his father-in-law, it's another to think about how that might play out in our lives. Getting advice from our family isn't always easy. But if we'll learn how to do it, we'll learn that our family can help us make some good decisions.

Option 2: Conflicting Advice. For this option, you need several Bibles, paper and pens or pencils. Read the following case study:

Leslie had a dilemma: This Saturday night was the county-wide band tournament, the school dance *and* the youth group overnighter at her church! She couldn't decide which to attend, so Leslie called her dad at work. His reply didn't really surprise her. "Les, honey," he said, "I'm sure you know that going to church is the best decision you could make. I'd like to see you go to the overnighter. You and your friends will get a lot out of it." Then he said he'd be home shortly and they could talk about it more then.

Leslie was still confused, so she found her mom, who was in the kitchen cooking dinner—typically a time when she did not like being distracted. Leslie gave her the scoop and she replied, "Leslie, you know that there are only so many band scholarships, dear. Every practice and performance counts. I think your church friends will understand. The best thing is for you to go to the tournament. Your father and I will discuss it more with you at dinner, okay?"

While Leslie was sitting on the couch contemplating her dilemma, Laurie, her sister, walked into the room. "Hey, Les, do you want to ride with Rob and me to the dance? His mom said there's plenty of room." Ugh! Leslie got even more confused and depressed with her sister's invitation.

Divide students into groups of three and distribute paper and pens or pencils to each group. Instruct students to discuss how Leslie should sort out the advice she's gotten so far from her family and to write down some things she could ask her family at dinner that night to help her make her decision.

Allow several minutes, and then have groups share what they've written. After each group has shared, distribute Bibles and discuss the following: "What should you do when you're not sure about your family's advice?" (*Pray about it before making a decision; have a family conference where everyone can give his or her opinion and insight.*)

Ask groups to read Proverbs 1:5; 12:15 and 19:20, and then discuss:

- How do these verses relate to Leslie's situation? *Leslie should listen to and consider the advice given to her by her family.*
- How might Leslie use these verses to come to a decision?

Youth Leader Tip

Giving teens the opportunity to talk about their families might provoke some students to talk negatively and critically. Be prepared to refocus attention back onto positive things about the students' parents, as well as proactive steps they can take to help out in their homes.

Explain to the group that getting advice from our families isn't always easy, but when we do, we can discover—just as Moses did—that our families can help us make some really good decisions.

APPLY

Option 1: Piece of Advice. For this option, you will need paper and pens or pencils.

Begin by explaining that every one of us has something we need to seek advice about from our families. Distribute paper and pens or pencils and ask students to think about the different aspects of their lives. (For example: school, home, friends, sports, band rehearsal, alone time.) Instruct them to draw a large circle on their papers and then to divide the circle into as many sections, or pie pieces, as there are facets of their lives and label each piece with one of those facets. Allow a few minutes for students to work.

Invite them to think of *one* area in which they need advice and have them write the advice they need in that section of the pie. (For example, students might write, "I need advice about homework," in the school section.) Ask for volunteers to share what they've written.

Instruct students to exchange papers and to pray silently for the owner of the paper they now have. After two minutes or so, ask everyone to return the papers to their owners. Conclude by stating that while going to our family for advice can be hard at times, we now have one thing that we can use to break the ice this week and ask advice for. Challenge students to approach their family for advice by the next group meeting, then close in prayer, asking God to provide opportunities for students to open up to their families with their need for advice.

Option: If you have the supplies, give each student a real pie pan (or paper plate) and have them use black felt-tip pens to write their ideas. If you're a leader with a whole bunch of time on your hands (and a small group!), bake each student a personal-size pie. Have them eat the pie; then use the empty pans to do this activity! (And if you have *that* much time, why not consider sending a pie to the author too?)

Option 2: God's Word of Advice. For this option, you need just this book.

Begin by explaining that it's often hard for junior-highers to go to their family for advice. It might just feel uncomfortable, or they might feel like the advice their family members give isn't good advice. However, they can encourage their friends in times like that by pointing them to someone who always gives perfect advice—God.

Ask students to shout out problems that junior-highers have and might need advice for. After each problem, pause and see if students can think of anything from the Bible that might relate to that problem. Be prepared to step in with references if students get stuck; if *you* get stumped, refer to Philippians 4:6, where we are encouraged not to be anxious but to take everything to God through prayer and thanksgiving!

Close in prayer, asking God to help students make *His* advice clear and appealing to those who don't know Him yet.

REFLECT

The following short devotions are for the students to reflect on and answer during the week. You can make a copy of these pages and distribute to your class or print out from the PDF available online at **www.gospellight.com/uncommon_jh_parents_and_family.zip**.

1—OUT IN THE COLD

Want to know how to succeed? Read Proverbs 15:22!

Paul really wanted to go camping in the woods behind his house one weekend in April. A *very* independent 13-year-old, he told his family that he didn't need any of the advice they offered on what to bring, what to wear or even where to camp. He was going to do it all by himself.

It turned out Paul didn't know much about camping—that's probably the reason he wore shorts and a thin T-shirt, and only brought a flimsy blanket and a pillow for sleeping and marshmallow-fluff sandwiches to eat. Needless to say, a cold and hungry Paul came back to the house before the night was through!

The next weekend, Paul wanted to give camping another try, and since he didn't want to make the same mistakes as last time, he asked his family for advice about how to do it best. Paul spent the night in a sleeping bag in a warm tent with a full belly, feeling very thankful that he had his family to help him figure things out.

A family can be a great source for advice. Do you turn to your family when you would like some help, or do you try to be tough and do it yourself? Why or why not?

_____

_____

_____

_____

_____

Many times, asking your family to help you figure something out can keep you from making mistakes and can help you make whatever it is you are trying to do run more smoothly. Thank God for your family in your prayers today and ask Him to help you remember your family as a great source of advice when you need it.

2—EXPLORING THE OPTIONS

Find Ecclesiastes 7:5 and listen up!

Imagine that you are trying to figure out what you should do with your summer. You decide to ask several people what they think you should do. Who would you listen to?

❑ Your friend Barry, who says you should spend the summer watching TV, skateboarding and eating candy bars and slushies

❑ Ann, a younger girl from church, who says you should sleep in every day and spend lots of time on the phone

❑ Steve, the little kid you baby-sit, who tells you to hang out with him all summer, finger painting and playing in his wading pool

❑ Your older sister, who suggests checking out that science camp you were interested in last summer but didn't have the time for

Do you ask your family to help you make decisions? Do you trust them when they give you advice? Why or why not?

_____

_____

_____

_____

_____

What is one wise thing someone in your family has told you recently?

_____

_____

_____

_____

_____

3—ON THE DEFENSIVE

Be quick to find James 1:19!

Kelly wanted to dye her hair black. "But, Kelly," her mom said when she asked for permission, "you have such pretty hair *now*. Don't you think you will look a little strange with black hair?"

Kelly blew her very nice brown bangs out of her eyes and said with a lot of attitude, "*Whatever*, Mom. So can I do it or not?"

Kelly's mom told her she would have to think about it. "You're pretty young to be dyeing your hair. I'm not sure how I feel about it. Ask me again in the morning."

This made Kelly *mad*. "Why can't you just decide *now*? You don't want me to have any fun at all!"

When your family tries to give you advice, do you listen? Or do you quickly become defensive? Explain.

_____

_____

_____

_____

_____

God wants us to listen to the wise people He has put into our lives. Try to be a good listener today—you may be surprised by what your family has to say!

4—MAKING CONNECTIONS

Hey you! What are you doing? Proverbs 19:20 is where it's at!

It had been a big day for Kristen. A really cute guy named Josh, who was a whole grade ahead of her, had asked her to go with him to a beach party next Saturday! She had a problem, though: She didn't know most of the people who would be there and didn't know exactly what the party would be like.

Kristen knew that she should talk with her parents to figure it out, but she hadn't been getting along too well with her mom lately, and her dad and stepmom were busy with their new baby. Check the action or actions Kristen should take:

- ❑ Just go to the party—it will probably be fine.
- ❑ Forget about the party—she didn't really want to go anyway.
- ❑ Ask her mom if they can spend some time together to work out their differences, and then ask for her mom's advice.
- ❑ Email her dad so that he can read about the situation at a convenient time, then follow-up with a call to get his opinion.

You'll get the best advice from your family when you make an effort to connect with them. What is one way you will connect with your family today?

_____

_____

_____

_____

_____

Sometimes family members don't know we need them until we let them know. Do you need some attention from your family? How will you tell them this week?

_____

_____

_____

_____

_____

GLUED TOGETHER OR TORN APART?

THE BIG IDEA

God's intent for marriage is for it to be permanent—but even when marriages end, He can heal families.

SESSION AIMS

In this session you will guide students to (1) understand the biblical perspective on divorce; (2) feel motivated to reach out in love to those who are affected by divorce right now; and (3) choose one way they can experience Christ's stability in the midst of being affected by a divorce.

THE BIGGEST VERSE

"Love is patient, love is kind. It does not envy, it does not boast, it is not proud. It is not rude, it is not self-seeking, it is not easily angered, it keeps no record of wrongs. Love does not delight in evil but rejoices with the truth. It always protects, always trusts, always hopes, always perseveres" (1 Corinthians 13:4-7).

OTHER IMPORTANT VERSES

Genesis 2:20-24; Matthew 19:4-9; 1 Corinthians 7:12-16; Philippians 2:1-4

Note: Additional options and worksheets in 8½" x 11" format for this session are available for download at **www.gospellight.com/uncommon_jh_parents_and_family.zip**.

Note: *This week's topic may be sensitive for some students in your group. Choose each section's options based on your group's particular needs, emphasizing different aspects of the topic depending on where your students are in heart and mind. You know your students best, so use what you know to shape this week's experience!*

STARTER

Option 1: Opening Questions. For this option, you need just this book!

Welcome students and introduce today's topic by letting them know that today you're going to talk about something that affects most of us, either directly or indirectly. The topic is divorce.

Divide students into pairs. Explain that you are going to ask a question and students are to share their answers with their partners. (The person with the longest hair can share first.) Ask, "Who do you know who has gone or who is going through a divorce?"

Allow a moment for answers to be exchanged, and then have students switch partners for the next question. (The person with the biggest thumb can share first.) Ask, "What happens to the rest of the family when parents divorce?"

Allow time for students to answer, then have them switch partners again. (The person standing closest to you can answer first.) Ask, "Why does divorce happen?"

You know the drill—have students switch for the final question. (This time, have the student whose next birthday is closest to today answer first.) Ask, "How do you think God feels about divorce?"

Explain to students that the last question was the most important one. How *does* God feel about divorce? Allow for responses; then continue by suggesting that it's important for us to know God's plan for marriage long before it's time to make that life-changing decision. When we are grounded in God's Word, we can commit to a life-long partner knowing that His will is for our marriage to last.

Option 2: Divorce Dilemmas 1. For this option, you need copies of "Divorce Dilemmas" (found on the next page) and pens or pencils. (*Note:* If you decide to use Option 2 in "Dig," you will want to group students in the same groups used in this option.)

Greet students and divide them into four groups. Distribute "Divorce Dilemmas" and pens or pencils. Explain to them that divorce is a pretty common thing these days—in fact, odds are that every person in this room has been

DIVORCE DILEMMAS

Situation 1

Jim's parents' divorce was final last month. Lately, he's been getting really angry at school. He's been yelling at teachers, pushing people into lockers—even experimenting with drugs. You've been Jim's best friend for the past four years and you really want to help him. What should you say?

Situation 2

Last night your parents announced that they're splitting up. You just stared blankly at them, not knowing what to say or how to react. After a while, you got up and went to your room and shut the door. You sat on your bed and knew you needed someone to talk to. You kept picking up the phone and dialing your cousin's number, and then hanging up before she could answer. You didn't even know what to say to her—or what you wanted her to say to you. Finally, you dialed and waited for her to answer. How did she react to the news?

Situation 3

Lately your parents have been fighting a lot. You've heard them late at night arguing about all sorts of things. Tonight (when your parents thought you were asleep) you heard your dad yell, "Fine, maybe I'll just leave then!" You really want to talk to someone about what you heard, so you call your youth pastor and make an appointment with her for tomorrow. What might you ask her? What might she say to you?

Situation 4

Your science teacher doesn't go to church, but he knows you're a Christian and has always been really nice to you. Today in class he announced that you're going to have a substitute teacher for a while. He said that he's going through a divorce, and he needs time to look for a new place to live. You're convinced that you need to say something to him; you want to convey your support and maybe suggest that he go to church. But you're not sure what to say. What should you do?

affected by it, either because their own parents are divorced or because someone they care about has gone through it. Ask groups to read the situations on
the handout and choose one to discuss.

Allow a few minutes for groups to respond, and then have them share
which situation they chose and their response to that situation. When all the
groups have shared, explain that today you're going to take a close look at divorce and learn what the Bible says about it. Ultimately, you're going to discover God's view of divorce and what they can do when they know someone
who is experiencing its effects.

MESSAGE

Option 1: God's Word on the D-Word. For this option, you need Bibles, four
large sheets of butcher paper or newsprint, a wide felt-tip pen, pens or pencils, masking or transparent tape, and 3x5-inch index cards.

Ahead of time, write each of the following Scripture references on a different piece of butcher paper or newsprint: Genesis 2:20-25; Deuteronomy
24:1-4; Matthew 19:4-9; 1 Corinthians 7:12-16. Also ahead of time, tape the
Scripture references in different locations around the room and place a stack
of index cards and pens or pencils at each location.[1]

Explain that the Bible has a lot to say about marriage and divorce. First, we
need to get an accurate picture of what the rules are, and then we'll look at
how we can apply them. Pair off students and distribute a Bible to each pair.
Explain that you've posted four Scripture references around the room and that
pairs are to work together to locate the posters. At each location, they should
look up each Scripture reference, write what they think the passage means on
an index card and leave the card facedown at the location. Then they may
move on to the next location.

Allow plenty of time for students to complete all four passages, then regroup and read one of the passages aloud. Ask a volunteer to walk over to the

Youth Leader Tip
You can make this more personal by inviting a
married person and a divorced person to come
and share their perspectives on marriage and
divorce. If possible, choose people with whom
your students are familiar, and share the outline
for the talk with them ahead of time.

poster for that passage and read what was written on the index cards. Continue until all four passages have been addressed, then discuss:

- What did you learn about divorce from these passages? *When they get married, a man and woman become one in God's eyes; God hates divorce.*

- Why do you think God has rules about divorce? *Without them, married people wouldn't honor each other and their commitment to each other would only last as long as they didn't have any difficulties.*

- In God's view, is divorce ever okay? *God feels very strongly about divorce. In fact, the Bible says He actually hates it (see Malachi 2:16). The only allowance He gives for it is when one of the people in the marriage is unfaithful (see Matthew 19:9).* (*Note:* Students may bring up the issue of abuse here—it can be argued that abuse is a violation of a marriage promise and therefore a form of unfaithfulness.)

Explain that the Bible has very firm ideas about what marriage is and what God's view of divorce is. When people divorce, it affects a lot more people than just the two getting divorced—and it's especially hard on any kids involved. Anyone who cares about the couple divorcing gets caught in the crossfire. Tell the group you're going to look at how we can help people who are affected by divorce.

Option 2: Marriage Laws. For this option, you need several Bibles, copies of "Marriage Laws" (found on the next page) and pens or pencils.

Explain to students that divorce is pretty common these days, and many churches are trying to figure out exactly what the Bible has to say about the subject. Distribute "Marriage Laws" and pens or pencils, and then divide students into groups of four. Tell them to imagine that they've been asked to give a report to your church about what laws from the Bible govern marriage. Allow time for students to complete the handouts, and then ask groups to present their findings. Discuss:

- What did you learn about divorce from reading these passages? *God's rules don't change and He has a definite opinion on divorce.*
- Why did God create marriage? *He understood the importance of companionship.*
- How do you think God feels when marriages break up? *He is not a happy camper!*

Marriage Laws

Read each of the following passages and then summarize what those verses have to say about marriage and divorce:

Genesis 2:20-24: _____
_____
_____
_____

Deuteronomy 24:1-4: _____
_____
_____
_____

Matthew 19:4-9: _____
_____
_____
_____

1 Corinthians 7:12-16: _____
_____
_____
_____

Ephesians 5:22-33: _____
_____
_____
_____

Conclude by pointing out that God's Word is clear about God's intention for marriage: that it would be a life-long commitment that brings blessing and honor to Him and to families. Divorce breaks God's heart because it hurts everyone involved. He didn't give us rules against divorce just to be bossy; He gave them to protect us from hurt, pain and heartbreak.

DIG

Option 1: D-I-V-O-R-C-E Support. For this option, you need several Bibles, paper and felt-tip pens.

Distribute paper and pens, then divide students into groups of four and ask them to write "D-I-V-O-R-C-E" across the long side of their papers. Explain to students that we've read God's law about divorce. Now we want to try to understand how it affects all sorts of people—the two who are splitting up, their parents, their children, their friends and a whole host of others.

Read 1 Corinthians 13:4-7 and explain that this passage has to do with loving others. Have them consider how they might show love to someone who is affected by a divorce.

Ask each group to think up seven ideas for loving a friend whose family is going through a divorce; each idea must begin with a different letter from the word "divorce." For example, for the first letter, students might write, "<u>D</u>on't let that person go to bed each night without an encouraging word." After a few minutes, ask some groups to share what they've written, then discuss:

- When might it be difficult to love someone who is affected by a divorce? *People react in a lot of different ways to divorce. Your best friend may act like she doesn't care about anything or anyone anymore—including God. Your cousin may be so angry that he's really unpleasant to be around. The key to loving someone who's going through such a difficult time is to understand that his or her behavior is a sign of the tremendous pain caused by the divorce. Your continued support will be a reminder that you care about what's happening and so does God.*

- Does loving someone who is experiencing the effects of a divorce mean that we are saying that divorce is okay? *Absolutely not! It does mean that we care about the people who are being affected by it.*

- What kinds of things do you think Jesus would say to someone whose parents are going through a divorce? *It's not your fault. You aren't responsible for decisions adults make. Remember, I love you and I am always here.*

- What would He do? *He would assure them of God's love for them and encourage them to turn to Him with their pain and confusion.*

Explain to the group that God doesn't like divorce—in fact, He hates it (see Malachi 2:16)—but He wants us ready and willing to care for and support anyone who is affected by it. Loving them is the key. If we can learn to love them as their parents are divorcing, they'll be encouraged.

Option 2: Divorce Dilemmas 2. For this option, you need an adult volunteer whose parents divorced when he or she was a young teen (or thereabouts), several Bibles, four copies of "Divorce Dilemmas" (found on page 43) and pens or pencils.

Ahead of time, ask an adult volunteer whose parents divorced when he or she was a young teen to share what he or she would have liked others to have done for him or her during the divorce.

Invite the adult volunteer to share his or her experience, making sure to cover the following questions: *How did other people you know respond to you when your parents were getting divorced? What do you wish they had done differently? What do you wish you had done differently?*

Divide students into four groups and distribute one copy of "Divorce Dilemmas" and a pen or pencil to each group. (*Note:* If you used option 2 in "Starter," group students into the same groups formed during that option for this discussion.)

Read 1 Corinthians 13:4-7, and then explain that you've talked a lot about what the Bible teaches about divorce. This passage clearly says that we're supposed to love each other *no matter what.* Assign each group a number from one to four and instruct the groups to read the situation on the handout that corresponds to that number. (*Note:* If you used option 2 in "Starter," assign groups a different situation than the one they completed in that option.) Each group should come up with at least five ways that they could show love to the person in the situation. Allow a few minutes for small-group discussions, and then invite each group to share its ideas. Discuss:

- What difference could this Bible passage make in how you treat someone in the midst of a divorce?
- What are some of the best ways to love people in this situation?

Explain that God doesn't like divorce—in fact, He hates it (see Malachi 2:16)—but He wants us ready and willing to care for and support those who are affected by it. He doesn't want us to run away from it. That means that if your parents are getting a divorce, you ought to ask your friends to be there for you and let them know how they can help you.

Finish this option by having students turn first to the person on their left, and then to the person on their right, to share one thing they've learned about how to help people going through divorce, based on 1 Corinthians 13:4-7.

APPLY

Option 1: Jesus Is My Rock. For this option, you need one rock per student (small enough to be handheld, but large enough to illustrate the stability of a rock). (*Option:* Have students use permanent felt-tip pens to write "Jesus is my Rock" on their rocks.)

Explain that every one of us has difficult things going on in our families. Statistically, approximately 40 percent of children in the United States have parents who are divorced.[2] The remaining percentage don't just glide through however—every family has its share of tough times, and sometimes our families can seem topsy-turvy and out of control.

Distribute a rock to each student and invite him or her to consider how strong and hard and stable it is—it doesn't change, no matter how much pressure they put on it. Explain that Jesus is like this rock; no matter what we're going through, He is the solid foundation we can rely on when everything else appears to be crumbling around us.

Close in prayer, thanking God for His strength and unchanging nature and asking Him to comfort students in the midst of the difficulties in their families (including divorce). Invite students to take their rocks home and place them in a prominent place in their bedrooms as a reminder to lean on God's strength and stability. Encourage them to continue building their lives on the rock of

Youth Leader Tip

It really doesn't matter what your theology of divorce is when you're in the presence of someone who's smack in the middle of it. They don't want to know your theological position on the subject—they just want to be loved. So love them!

Jesus; when it comes time for them to marry, they can commit with confidence, knowing that relationships grounded in Christ will last.

Option 2: The Touch of Jesus' Love. For this option, you need your Bible, several black felt-tip pens, a 2x4 board approximately three feet long and something to support the board at the base so that it can stand upright (you can build a small base or use sand bags, rocks or books).

Ahead of time, support the board so that it stands upright (it needs to be pretty secure) and place the pens at the base. (*Option:* Lay the board on a table or even on the floor so that students can write on it; then, when they have finished writing, prop it up.)

Read Philippians 2:1-4 and explain that the Bible is very clear about what we must do for people who are experiencing hardship in their families: We're supposed to support them. We don't have to agree with what's going on, but we must make every effort to love and support them.

Ask students to gather around the board. Invite them to use the pens to write the initials of or draw a picture to represent someone they know who is experiencing divorce or hardship in his or her family. When everyone is finished, have students find another person's initials or drawing and place their hands on it. Explain that what they are doing now is exactly what the Bible asks us to do: touch those people with Jesus' love. Invite students who are comfortable praying aloud for the people represented on the board to do so. Then close in prayer, thanking God for allowing us to support and love one another in times of crisis and asking Him to show students ways they can show His love to someone who is having a hard time during the next week.

REFLECT

The following short devotions are for the students to reflect on and answer during the week. You can make a copy of these pages and distribute to your class or print out from the PDF available online at **www.gospellight.com/ uncommon_jh_parents_and_family.zip**.

1—THE DOWNSIDE OF FREE WILL

Who cares? Read 1 Peter 5:6-7 to find out!

Lane lived with his mom every other week. For some reason, she made him go to church. Lane was convinced that he hated it more than *any* kid on earth. He hated getting up early and he always forgot to eat breakfast. There he was: stuck in church all morning, feeling tired and hungry.

The worst part was that Lane hated what he kept hearing—all about how God loved him and if Lane were obedient to Him, life would be good. Well, life hadn't been so great for Lane lately and it wasn't even his fault. His parents, who had always fought like crazy, got a divorce last year. Lane hadn't worried about it too much then—in fact, he was even kind of glad because he thought their fighting would at least stop. Boy, was he *wrong*. Things were even worse now—his parents fought when they were anywhere near each other and they couldn't agree on anything.

Lane was miserable and thought to himself, *How can God care about me but let this junk happen? I didn't do anything to deserve this!*

When things are going badly, sometimes it's tempting to blame God and think that He's not being fair. But here's the truth: Other people's bad decisions are not God's fault. When others hurt you, God wants to comfort you and help you grow strong through the experience. He can use even the worst circumstances—like a divorce—to draw you closer to Him. Ask God to help you trust Him more today with what He is doing in your life.

2—DECISIONS, DECISIONS

How ya doin'? Flip to Philippians 4:4-7 right now!

Let's say your parents got divorced a couple of years ago and today your mom sat you down on her bed and announced that she had something important to tell you. You couldn't believe it when she said that she'd decided to move to a new state—and that it's up to you to decide whether you will keep living with her or move in with your dad and his new wife. What do you do?

❑   Run to your room, climb under the covers of your bed and refuse to come out until your mom promises not to move.

❑   Yell, "It's not fair!" and slam the door as you run out of the house.

❑   Nod, go into your room and pray; then call up some of the wise people you know and ask for advice about what you should do.

There's no way around it—divorce stinks! If your parents are going through (or have already gone through) a divorce, there are many decisions that you may have to make. How do you react when you have a hard decision to make? Do you overreact? Do you get angry and blame people? Do you turn to God?

_____

_____

_____

_____

_____

What do you think God wants you to do about it this week?

_____

_____

_____

_____

3—HEAVENLY DAD

Who's your Daddy? Psalm 68:4-5 will tell you!

Liam's dad had left and moved to another country when Liam was less than a year old. He never tried to get in touch with Liam, and Liam never really tried to get in touch with him, either.

Liam didn't miss his dad very much—after all, he didn't know him at all. Sometimes, though, he felt cheated when he needed some help with his homework, needed some advice or needed a ride somewhere and his mom was too busy or too tired—or simply not there—to help him. And there were some nights Liam just lay in his bed, thinking how different his life would be if his father had stayed and imagining what kind of man his father really was.

Even if a child doesn't really know his or her parent, not having him or her around leaves kind of a hole where the parent should be. God wants to fill that hole and care for us as our heavenly Father. Ask Him to be the Dad you need.

What does it mean to you to have God as your heavenly Father?

_____

_____

_____

_____

4—HARD TO LOVE

Find Ephesians 5:1-2 and be an imitator!

Okay, let's say that your dad just got remarried to a nice woman. Unfortunately, her kids aren't nice *at all*. You and these kids didn't get along when your dad and their mom were dating—and now they are going to come and live in your house! What do you do?

- ❑ Set strict rules for them like, "Never, *ever* talk to me" and "Never, *ever* touch my stuff."
- ❑ Scare them into becoming your servants.
- ❑ Be as nice as possible, even when you feel like screaming at them.
- ❑ Moan and groan and complain constantly to your dad about how much you can't stand the kids, and beg him to send them away to boarding school.

How does God want you to treat the people who are hardest for you to love?

_____

_____

_____

_____

Are you always the easiest person in the world to love? Why or why not?

_____

_____

_____

_____

How does God want you to treat the people who are hardest for you to love?

_____

_____

_____

_____

CLOSER THAN YOU THINK

THE BIG IDEA

No matter what your earthly father is like, God is your heavenly Father who loves you dearly.

SESSION AIMS

In this session you will guide students to (1) discover that God wants to have relationships with them that are better than any other; (2) feel motivated to develop their relationship with God; and (3) commit to having a more active relationship with God.

THE BIGGEST VERSE

"'Abba, Father,' he said, 'everything is possible for you. Take this cup from me. Yet not what I will, but what you will'" (Mark 14:36).

OTHER IMPORTANT VERSES

Mark 14:32-42; Romans 8:12-17; Galatians 4:1-7

Note: Additional options and worksheets in 8¹/₂" x 11" format for this session are available for download at **www.gospellight.com/uncommon_jh_parents_and_family.zip**.

STARTER

Option 1: A Great Debate. For this option, you need a stopwatch and three adult volunteers to serve as spokespersons for a debate. (*Note:* This option requires a fair amount of theological background, which might be beyond your volunteers'—and maybe even your own—training. If it is, choose one of the other great options.)

Ahead of time, ask the debaters to brainstorm arguments and examples to support the following statements (let them know that their arguments should have at least some element of truth, but they can include some ridiculous elements, too):

- A relationship with God is possible only if you're perfect.
- God chooses popular people to have a relationship with.
- Once you have a relationship with God, all your problems are solved.
- Satan doesn't care if you have a strong relationship with God.

Greet students and introduce the debaters. Explain that you're going to read four statements, one at a time. When you read a statement, each debater will have one minute to provide his or her arguments and examples to support the validity of the statement.

After the debate, invite students to point out any arguments that had some truth to them, as well as anything that sounded totally false; then dive into the lesson by explaining that there are a lot of myths that surround having a relationship with God. It's easy to have some misguided impressions of what it means to have a relationship with our heavenly Father, partly because of the problems we may experience with our earthly parents. Tell them that today they're going to discover how they can have a relationship with God—who is, as they'll see, pretty different from their earthly parents.

Option 2: Difficult Match. For this option, you need copies of "Difficult Match" (found on the following page), pens or pencils and one copy of "Difficult Match Answers" (found on page 58). Ahead of time, tape "Difficult Match Answers" in a prominent place.

Greet students and have them sit in a circle. Distribute "Difficult Match" and pens or pencils and announce that students have five minutes to complete the handout.

If you notice students having a difficult time during the five minutes, *very loudly* state, "Answers are often closer than you think. They're *really* close. It's

Difficult Match

Draw a line to match the scientific name on the
left with its common name on the right.

Musca domestica	Hercules beetle
Latrodectus mactans	black locust
Robinia pseudoacacia	monarch butterfly
Bufo baxteri	European honeybee
Danaus plexippus	black widow spider
Litoria infrafrenata	red ant
Apis mellifera	giant tree frog
Pogonomyrmex barbatus	common housefly
Dynastes hercules	silkworm moth
Bombyx mori	Wyoming toad

Difficult Match
Answers

Musca domestica = common housefly

Notophthalmus viriclescens = red spotted newt

Latrodectus mactans = black widow spider

Robinia pseudoacacia = black locust

Bufo baxteri = Wyoming toad

Danaus plexippus = monarch butterfly

Litoria infrafrenata = giant tree frog

Apis mellifera = European honeybee

Pogonomyrmex barbatus = red ant

Dynastes hercules = Hercules beetle

Bombyx mori = silkworm moth

almost as though they're visible; as if you can see them from where you are." If students still don't get it, you might want to point out where you've taped the answers!

Allow several minutes, then (if you haven't done it already) point out the answers and explain that the answers to this game were in plain sight, but because they weren't looking for them, they didn't see them. Having a relationship with God is similar: He's so close, yet sometimes we don't recognize Him. Explain that today they're going to discover how close God really is and how they can have a relationship with our perfect heavenly Father.

MESSAGE

Option 1: Drama in Gethsemane. For this option, you need your Bible and (optional) skit costumes. Ahead of time, familiarize yourself with Mark 14:32-42 so you can help students act out the passage.

Divide students into five groups and assign each group to act as one of the following people in the passage: Peter, James, John, Jesus and the disciples (the rest of the group). Ask groups to act out the person's actions as a group as you read the passage. For instance, if the passage says that their character(s) falls asleep, they all sleep. Have each group gather in a different part of the meeting room, then begin reading Mark 14:32-42. When you've finished the passage, discuss the following:

- Why was Jesus feeling so troubled? *He knew that the time of His painful crucifixion was near and that it would cause Him incredible agony.*
- What did Jesus mean by "the cup"? *It was a metaphor for the terrible punishment and death that He was about to experience.*
- What did Jesus know about God that motivated Him to pray in this difficult time? *That God was always there for Him and that His will would be best, even though it would be painful.*
- How might you have felt if you were one of the disciples and Jesus found you sleeping? *Ashamed, embarrassed, and so on.*

Explain that it's interesting that Jesus calls God "Abba," which, in the ancient language, means "Daddy" or "Papa." This was a term that the Jews in His time would never use to address God, because to them it would have seemed disrespectful. But Jesus knew something that we sometimes forget: that God is much closer to us than we realize. (*Note:* If students aren't enthusiastic about acting, consider having just five or six students act out the passage [the four main characters, plus one or two as disciples]; then involve the audience in the discussion.)

Option 2: Potent Love and Trust. For this option, you need several Bibles, a brown paper bag, a sealable plastic bag, a fresh onion, a sharp knife, blank adhesive labels, felt-tip pens and a poster board. Ahead of time, use the poster board and a felt-tip pen to create a large sign with the word "God" on it. Cut the onion in half and place both halves in the plastic bag; seal the bag and place it in the paper bag.

Read Mark 14:32-42. Explain that Jesus had a very close relationship with God. Although it appears that His earthly father had died by the time Jesus began His ministry, He still could have cried out for Joseph in His agony—or even for His mother, Mary. Instead, during His last hours on earth, Jesus called out to His heavenly Father for comfort and strength—and by His submission to the will of His Father, Jesus showed us what it means to trust God, even to death.

Hold up the brown paper bag. Invite a few students to come forward and try to guess what's inside by smelling the outside of the bag. When they can't guess, give a hint: "There's something very potent in this bag, but until I tell you what it is, you won't know for sure."

Place your hand inside the outer bag and open the seal on the plastic bag without showing students what's inside. Invite the same students to smell the outside of the bag and try to guess what's inside again—something all should be able to do now. Point out that the difference this time was that they were actually exposed to the onion's potency, which was evident even without actually touching the onion itself. Explain that we can know God just as Jesus did—and the key is allowing Him to show us the potency and wonder of His love for us by opening the door and inviting Him in.

Next, read Mark 14:32-42 again. Explain that in the Garden of Gethsemane Jesus called to "Abba," which showed His total trust in God as His heavenly Father.

Distribute adhesive labels and pens and ask students to write one thing on their label that Jesus prayed and trusted God for in the garden; then have them place their label on the "God" poster board. After all the labels have been placed on the board, read through them and explain that we can trust in God for the same things Jesus did.

Finally, read Mark 14:32-42 *one more time*! Explain that Jesus' trust in God was reflected in His submission to God and His will—even if His will was to allow Jesus to go through an extremely painful death on the cross. We can make the same choice Jesus did, trusting in God to be in charge of every detail of our lives and submitting to His will, regardless of how uncomfortable (and sometimes painful) following His will can be.

DIG

Option 1: Words in Common. For this option, you need several Bibles, paper, pens or pencils and candy prizes.

Explain that we've seen how Jesus addressed God as "Daddy" or "Papa." What about us? Can we have that kind of intimate relationship with our heavenly Father? Tell students that they are going to take a look at what God says about *them* and their relationship with Him in the Bible.

Divide the students into groups of four and distribute Bibles and a piece of paper and a pen or pencil to each group. Instruct the groups to make two columns lengthwise and then write "Romans 8:12-17" on the left side of the paper and "Galatians 4:1-7" on the right side at the top. Then give each of the groups two minutes to see how many words they can find in common in the two passages (counting anything from "the" to something more complicated like "heir" or "slave").

Allow two minutes; then ask groups to share their answers and award candy to the group that found the most words in common. Point out the following five words in both passages (at least in the *NIV* Bible):

- *Slave:* Those who live according to their sinful natures are slaves to sin and fear.
- *Abba, Father:* God sends the Holy Spirit into our hearts so that we can call Him "Abba," just as Jesus did in the Garden of Gethsemane.
- *Sons, children:* We can call our Father "Abba" because God has redeemed us from the law and given us His Spirit so that we can become members of His family.
- *Heir:* When we live by the Spirit, we become His heirs, which means that we inherit eternal life and share in His glory.

Make sure students understand the passages by discussing:

- Who is God's child according to these passages? *Those who are led by the Spirit of God and are not slaves to sin.*

- What are the benefits of being God's children? *We have "full rights of sons" (Galatians 4:5), we have the Holy Spirit of Christ leading us, and we have eternal life.*

Option 2: Inside the Fence. For this option, you need several Bibles and this book. Introduce the following case study by explaining that it illustrates our ability to have a close relationship with God, just as Jesus did.

In World War II, a group of soldiers had a friend die. Wanting to give their friend a decent burial, they found a church with a graveyard behind it, surrounded by a white picket fence. They found the parish priest and asked if their friend could be buried there in the church graveyard.

"Was he Catholic?" the priest inquired.

"No, he was not," answered the soldiers.

"I'm sorry then," said the priest. "Our graveyard is reserved for members of the Holy Church. But you can bury your friend outside the fence. I will see that the gravesite is cared for."

"Thank you, Father," said the soldiers, and they proceeded to bury their friend just outside the graveyard on the other side of the fence.

When the war had finally ended, and before the soldiers returned home, they decided to visit the gravesite of their friend. They remembered the location of the church—and of the grave, just outside the fence. They searched for it, but couldn't find it. Finally, they went to the priest to inquire as to its location.

"Sir, we cannot find our friend's grave," said the soldiers to the priest.

"Well," answered the priest, "after you buried your fallen friend, it just didn't seem right to me that he should be buried there, outside the fence."

"So you moved his grave?" asked the soldiers.

"No," said the priest. "I moved the fence."[1]

Discuss the following:

- What in our lives represents the fence that keeps us from having a relationship with God in the first place? *Our sin, which is our going astray from God's will and which causes us to experience grief and guilt before a holy and righteous God.*

- How does this story relate to the way our heavenly Father reaches out to us? *Our sin puts us outside the fence—accepting Jesus as our Savior is God's way of moving the fence!*

Read Romans 8:12-17 and Galatians 4:1-7 aloud and use the information on the five common words outlined in the previous option to explain about what we inherit as a result of becoming God's children.

APPLY

Note: This step deals with comparing our heavenly Father to our earthly fathers. This can present difficulties for students who have had bad experiences (or no experience at all) with their earthly fathers, preventing them from perceiving God's love for them as their heavenly Father. Before proceeding with an option, let students know that you're going to lead them in a short prayer; those whose situations with their earthly fathers might hinder their view of God as their loving heavenly Father can repeat the following prayer, and those whose earthly fathers have had a positive influence on their lives can agree as you pray.

Dear Father, sometimes it can be hard to think of You as a loving Father because of my own experience with my earthly dad. Please send Your Holy Spirit into my heart and remove the roadblocks that keep me from accepting Your love for me as Your precious child. Amen.

Option 1: Close to the Father. For this option, you'll need blank paper, pens or pencils and two stickers per student (two different-colored dot stickers will work best).

Ask students to silently consider what their answers would be to the following questions: How do you view God? Is He a heavenly Father for you? Do you realize how close He is to you? Or do you view Him as less accessible?

Distribute paper, pens or pencils and stickers (one of each color to each student), and then have students draw a large cross in the center of their papers. Explain that this cross represents how Jesus died for us to take away our sin—the sin that keeps us from God, the Father. Because He died and was raised again, we now have the way back to having a relationship with God—a way to overcome the obstacle of our sin.

Have students place a sticker somewhere on the paper to show where they were with God when they walked into this room—how close they felt to Him or how far they felt from Him.

Allow a moment for students to place their stickers, and then explain that you're going to give them an opportunity to move closer to God. Invite them to spend a few minutes in silent prayer, either asking Jesus to take over their lives for the first time, or if they've done that already, asking God to help them know how close He is and show them ways to draw closer to Him. After a few moments of silent prayer, ask students to place a different-colored sticker on the cross to show how close they feel to God right now.

Close in prayer, thanking God for giving us a way back to Him through Jesus Christ and asking Him to show students ways that they can respond to His wonderful love.

Option 2: My Two Fathers. For this option, you will need several adult volunteers, copies of "My Two Fathers" (found on the following page) and pens or pencils.

Distribute "My Two Fathers" and pens or pencils and explain that there are some ways that our earthly dads are like God and some ways they aren't. Instruct students to spread out around the room and complete their handouts individually. Have them write several ways that their earthly fathers are similar to our heavenly Father and several ways that the two are different.

Allow three to five minutes for students to work, and then divide them into groups of three or four. Ask the adult volunteers to facilitate brief small-group discussions on what students wrote on their handouts.

After several minutes, regroup and explain that sometimes our relationship with our heavenly Father is actually hindered because of how we view our earthly fathers. Let students know that if this has been the case with any of them, you're going to give them an opportunity right now to recommit their life to Christ and renew their relationship with God. Invite students to repeat the following prayer after you:

Dear God, thank You so much for being my perfect Father. Forgive me for viewing a relationship with You as equal to my imperfect relationship with my earthly father. Please help me to come back to You and realize how close You are to me, what a perfect Father You are, and how much You love me. Amen.

MY 2 FATHERS

Use the chart below to list the similarities and differences between your earthly father and your heavenly Father.

Earthly father similarities	Heavenly Father similarities
Earthly father differences	Heavenly Father differences

REFLECT

The following short devotions are for the students to reflect on and answer during the week. You can make a copy of these pages and distribute to your class or print out from the PDF available online at **www.gospellight.com/ uncommon_jh_parents_and_family.zip**.

1—WHAT KIND OF GOD?

Hey, kiddo! Go find Romans 8:12-17!
   How do you picture God?

- ❏ He has a big white beard and says "thee" and "thou" and "shall not" all the time.
- ❏ He's a mean person who doesn't like me very much.
- ❏ He's a magic genie that I can go to with all of my problems, and He just makes them disappear.
- ❏ He wears a "World's Greatest Dad" hat and loves me like crazy.

How does God describe Himself to you—what kind of guy is He? Do you see Him the way He wants you to see Him?

_____
_____
_____
_____

How does your relationship with God change when you think about Him as a dad?

_____
_____
_____
_____

How can you help yourself remember that God is your Father this week?

_____
_____
_____
_____

2—TALK TO DAD

Go read Isaiah 58:11. Does it seem hot in here to you?

Chris sat on the beach, staring out at the ocean. It was a sweltering, hot day, yet the water was icy cold—too cold to swim in. Chris was feeling low and she dug her feet into the hot sand as she thought about her life.

So much had changed since she started junior high. School was a lot harder and she had very few friends in her classes. At home, she seemed to fight with her family every day and spent most of her time in her room, drawing and listening to the radio.

Chris looked up and saw a group of kids nearby playing Frisbee. She wished someone would ask her if she'd like to play too, but no one did. Sighing, she brought her knees up to her chest and looked out at the water again.

What types of things do you struggle with? Loneliness? Stress? Your family? Do you tell God what's going on in your life and ask Him to help you? Why or why not?

_____

_____

_____

_____

Have a long talk with God today and tell Him what is going on in your life and ask Him for help. Write a few sentences of your prayer below.

_____

_____

_____

_____

3—KNOCK, KNOCK

Hunt down 1 Timothy 1:15-17. It's somewhere near the back of the Book.

Imagine that you're sitting in your room. You've been waiting for your friend to come over when you hear a knock on the door. What do you do?

❑   Sit quietly and don't move, hoping whoever it is will go away.

❑   Snarl, "Go away!"

❑   Sit there and wait for the person knocking to open the door without an invitation.

❑   Yell, "Come in!" and jump up to open the door.

Jesus knocks on the door of your heart all the time, waiting for you to answer and let Him in. Do you want Him to come in? Is He already living in your heart? Having Jesus in your life can mean some pretty serious and wonderful changes. If you haven't already let Him in, or if you feel as if you haven't been letting Him stay in, pray this simple prayer: "*God, I believe You sent Your Son, Jesus, to die on the cross for my sins and that He came back to life three days later. Please come and live in my heart today and be my Savior and Lord.*"

Hey, if you just prayed that prayer for the first time, go call a friend who loves Jesus and celebrate!

4—FREE!

Read 1 Peter 2:23-25 and let freedom ring!

Chloe couldn't believe what was happening with her friends. On Monday, she had been so excited to tell them that she had become a Christian on Sunday morning at her friend's church and how happy she was! She was *not* prepared for her friends' reactions.

Her friend Dillon was the first—and the loudest—to react. "Oh *man*, Chloe! What'd you go and do a dumb thing like that for?! Now you can't smoke, you can't cuss—you can't do *anything*! You're gonna have the most *boring* life now! Geez!"

Chloe was surprised and replied, "But, Dillon, don't you get it? It's not that I don't *get* to do that stuff anymore; I don't *have* to do it! I've got something way better in my life now!"

When we become Christians, God frees us from our old lives! How cool is that? Living in sin drags us down and makes it hard for us to be happy and to get to know God and what He wants for us.

Spend five minutes in prayer today reminding yourself of how great it is that, because you know God, you are free from your old ways of sin. Woo-hoo!

WHO'S FIRST?

THE BIG IDEA

Putting God first does not mean dishonoring your parents.

SESSION AIMS

In this session you will guide students to (1) understand that no matter how imperfect families and parents are, God has placed their families together to bring honor to Him; (2) feel motivated to place Jesus first, even before family loyalty; and (3) seek guidance from responsible adults during times when they believe they are facing the choice between obeying their parents or following Jesus.

THE BIGGEST VERSE

"Honor your father and your mother, so that you may live long in the land the LORD your God is giving you" (Exodus 20:12).

OTHER IMPORTANT VERSES

Exodus 20:12; Matthew 19:16-30; Philippians 3:7-14; James 1:22-25

Note: Additional options and worksheets in 8^1/$_2$" x 11" format for this session are available for download at **www.gospellight.com/uncommon_jh_parents_and_family.zip**.

STARTER

This step helps students identify some of the decisions involved in placing God first in their lives and obeying Him.

Option 1: Interview with a Former Junior-Higher. For this option, you need a TV and a video camera. (*Low-tech option:* use an audio recorder.)

Ahead of time, make arrangements to interview an adult who is well known to students, such as the senior pastor or another member of the pastoral team. Record a two-part interview wherein the adult first shares about a time during junior high when he or she struggled with obedience (such as to his or her parents, a teacher or a school principal) and then, second, shares how the issue was resolved. Also ahead of time, prepare a list of three to five possible outcomes to the issue. (You can include the real outcome, but don't make it obvious.)

Welcome students and explain that you're going to start today by hearing from someone who remembers what it's like to be a junior-higher trying to figure out what to do. Show the first part of the video, and then instruct students to listen as you read each possible outcome to the situation. If they believe an outcome you read to be the real one, they are to move to the wall to your left. If they believe it to be false, they are to move to the wall to your right. If you have time, read the options again and have students move according to what they believe the person *should* have done. Show the second part of the video wherein the interviewee shares the outcome, then discuss:

- What is obedience? *It's the willingness to obey and follow orders.*
- How was obedience involved in this person's situation?
- What people and things should we obey in our lives? *Parents, teachers and others God has placed in authority over us. We also need to obey laws and rules, traffic signs, and so forth.*
- On a scale of 1 to 10 (10 being most important), how important is it that we obey our friends? *We should honor our friends, but we don't have to obey them because they are not placed in authority over us by God.*
- How about our families? *We should obey our parents and our elders because God has placed them in authority over us.*
- What if my parents tell me to do something that's illegal or goes against God? *That's pretty extreme, but unfortunately it can happen. If you're put in that position, the first thing you should do is to seek the counsel of a trustworthy Christian adult who can advise you on how to handle the situation with respect for your parents, while honoring God.*

Explain to the group that it may surprise them, but as they're going to see today, Jesus said that there is one thing we should put before everything else, even before our families.

Option 2: Competing for Obedience. For this option, you need copies of "Competing for Obedience" (found on the next page), pens or pencils and candy for prizes.

Welcome students, then distribute "Competing for Obedience" and pens or pencils. Explain that when you give the signal, students are going to fill out their handouts by following the directions for each square they choose. Once the action for a square is completed successfully, the square can be marked. When a student has three squares in a row marked, he or she should shout "Bingo!" and the game will end.

Give the signal to begin and watch carefully so you'll be able to identify the winner. When you have a winner, congratulate him or her and distribute the candy prizes to everyone as a reward for their efforts, then discuss:

- What is obedience? *It's doing what is asked—following orders.*
- If you had to make a list of things or people that you should obey, what might be on that list? *School rules; federal, state and local laws; God's commandments; parents; teachers; and so on.*
- What do you do if two people you're supposed to obey are telling you to do different things? *Explain to each one that you are confused about their instructions and ask them to clarify what they mean. You could also ask a third person for help.*

Explain that if someone is telling you one thing and God is telling you another, it can still be hard to know what to do. Today we'll see what advice Jesus gave about what to do.

Youth Leader Tip
Encourage students to seek the guidance of an older Christian before making any drastic changes in their lifestyles or home lives, and explain the difference between turning one's back on family and standing up for one's belief in Jesus Christ.

COMPETING FOR OBEDIENCE

The object of the game is to connect three boxes vertically, horizontally or diagonally. Find a person in the group for whom one of the boxes' statements are true, and have them sign their name. Each person can only sign one box!

Find someone who obeyed his or her parents in the last 24 hours.	Find someone who has struggled with obeying a commandment.	Find someone who will spell O-B-E-D-I-E-N-C-E out loud with you, each person alternating letters.
Find someone who has argued with his or her parents in the last week.	FREEBIE!	Find someone who can tell you three of his or her family's rules.
Find someone who has a friend who has argued with his or her parents in the last week.	Find someone who will say "Obey God in all things" 10 times very fast.	Find someone who can recite five of the Ten Commandments without looking at the Bible.

MESSAGE

Option 1: Spinning Bat Relay. For this option, you need several Bibles, several baseball bats, masking tape (or string and something to secure it to the ground), candy and soda.

Ahead of time, locate a large area where students can run around (ideally a grass field or a large, carpeted room—asphalt is too rough for this game!) and use tape or string to mark starting and finish lines for the game. Also ahead of time, practice the activity yourself so that you can demonstrate!

Direct students to the area that you've selected for the game, and then divide them into the number of teams equal to the number of baseball bats you have. Instruct each team to line up single file behind the starting line and explain the rules: One person at a time from each team will run to the finish line and pick up a bat. Then, hold the handle of the bat up to your forehead (so it's sticking out like a unicorn's horn) and put the other end on the ground; then spin around 10 times. After 10 spins, run back to the starting line—note that the next person in line *can't go* until you've crossed the line. The team that finishes first wins candy *and* sodas. Everybody else gets a soda. (If you haven't figured it out already, students are going to be hopelessly dizzy and running back to their teams is going to be a challenge—but hey, that's the fun of the game!)

After the game is over and everyone has enjoyed their treats, regroup and explain that often we're motivated to do things, especially hard or unfamiliar things like the spinning bat relay, because of what we know we're going to get out of it (in this case, candy and soda). People in the Bible were a lot like us. They were willing to do something difficult if they knew there would be some kind of reward for what they did.

Distribute Bibles and ask for a volunteer to read Exodus 20:12. Explain that "honor your father and your mother" is one of the Ten Commandments. It comes right after the commandments about honoring and worshiping God, so we know that He thinks it's very important. In the Bible, "to honor" means to prize and cherish, to care for, to show respect for and, yes, to obey. This applies not just to children, but also to adults who honor their parents by caring for them in their old age.

Continue by saying, "Let's compare the command to honor our parents with the story of a rich young man told in Matthew 19:16-30." Read the passage, then explain that this guy was really bummed out because although he was willing to obey the commandments, he didn't want to give up his possessions on earth to live eternally in the kingdom of heaven.

Now discuss the following:

- What did the man's possessions represent in this story? *His reluctance to trust God to provide everything he would need.*
- Why did the disciples ask Jesus what there was for them after leaving everything behind to follow Him? *They followed Jesus willingly, but they wondered if they would be rewarded in heaven for their sacrifices.*

Conclude by telling students that we can usually obey God and our families at the same time, but the absolute commitment required to be a disciple of Jesus might sometimes mean that other things—even things that might be fun, like participating in a family activity—have to be sacrificed. In extreme cases, when we are faced with totally disobeying our parents in order to follow Jesus, it's best to seek the advice of a trustworthy Christian adult who can help us to figure out how to honor and respect our parents and still follow God's will. Sometimes obeying God is tough; however, think about what we'll end up with—eternal life in heaven with our Lord and Savior!

Option 2: Smash 'Em! For this option, you need one small watermelon, cantaloupe, honeydew or pumpkin (or any other similar fruit that looks messy when smashed), a plastic tarp, a sledgehammer, paper, pens or pencils and a few black felt-tip pens.

Read Matthew 19:23-27, and then explain that we have to be ready to leave everything to follow Christ. Jesus asks us to clear out everything that stands in the way of our following Him. In His encounter with the rich young man, He brings out the point that whatever we hold as valuable can keep us from obeying God and doing His will.

Hold up the watermelon and explain that it represents our favorite possessions. Ask students to come forward and take turns writing their favorite possessions on the outside of the watermelon with the felt-tip pens. When everyone has had a chance to write his or her possession, explain that you're going to show them what Jesus wants us to do with our possessions.

Place the watermelon on the plastic and smash it with the sledgehammer. Point out that this is the view Jesus wants us to have of the things we own; the importance of our possessions pales in comparison to our relationship with Him.

Next, read Matthew 19:28-30, and then explain that Jesus clearly explains to His disciples that there's a reward for obeying and following Him wholeheartedly, even if it means placing Him ahead of our families.[1]

Distribute paper and markers, and then ask students to draw a picture of their families. (They can just draw stick figures if they want.) Then invite them to write a few things above each picture that they appreciate about each family member. When everyone has finished writing, have students wad up the pictures and throw them at you (*duck!*).

Explain that this is a very drastic illustration, but it's exactly what Jesus is telling His disciples. They can love their families, but they've got to place Him above all else. When we give our lives to Jesus, we become part of a new family, and Jesus provides everything we need.

Finally, read Exodus 20:12, and explain that honoring God is the most important thing we can do with our lives. When we honor and respect our parents, we please God by showing that we recognize that He has, in His divine wisdom and knowledge, placed us in our particular families—sometimes for reasons only He knows! It is entirely possible to show respect to our parents and reject their belief system when it goes against following Jesus Christ. To do this takes some wise counsel from other mature Christians, though, so it's important not to make any rash decisions when we don't agree with our parents.

DIG

Option 1: Case Studies. For this option, you need several Bibles and the following for every four to six students: one copy of "Case Studies" (found on the next page), pens or pencils and several 3x5-inch index cards.

Divide students into groups of four to six. Then explain that putting God first is a nice idea, and it's easy to read about people who needed to obey God in the Bible, but what about obeying God in the real world? Is it really possible?

Distribute a copy of "Case Studies" and a pen or pencil to each group, and then assign each group one of the case studies. (Depending on the number of students you have, some studies may be assigned to more than one group.) Each group should read its study and come up with advice for the person in the situation. Allow a few minutes for brainstorming, and then invite each group to share briefly the advice they would give the person from their case study.

Explain that God wants us to obey Him because it's part of His plan for us. If we obey Him, we'll be able to know His will and obey it. Let's check out what the Bible says about obeying God.

Distribute a Bible and two index cards to each group. Instruct groups to read Philippians 3:7-14 and James 1:22-25 and then write down on an index card what each passage means, along with the Scripture reference. Allow a few

Case Studies

Case Study 1

Linda and Jen are really close friends; they borrow each other's clothes, talk on the phone for hours and can't stand to be apart. Earlier this week, Linda called Jen, crying.

"Jen, you'll never believe this," she sobbed. "My parents have signed me up for *swimming* lessons."

"What's so wrong with that?" Jen asked.

"Practice is at the same time as church! My dad said that I have to sacrifice time at church to work out and make the swim team. My mom says she did it, so I should too. They don't care about what matters to me!"

What advice should Jen give Linda?

Case Study 2

Your older sister, Stephanie, has tried it all—drugs, alcohol, you name it. You've been praying for her ever since you accepted Jesus three years ago . . . and just last week, she actually asked if she could go to youth group with you!

The night she went, your youth pastor had a guest speaker share his testimony. Your sister was so moved by his story that she decided to give her life to Jesus. Since that night, she's been reading her Bible and tonight she started attending a Bible study.

Two hours after curfew, Stephanie came home to find your parents waiting for her. You were in bed, but you could still hear their conversation from your room.

"Stephanie, where have you been?!"

"I'm sorry, Mom, we got carried away at Bible study tonight. I learned some really neat stuff!"

"I'm glad you've decided to be closer to God, Steph, but you still need to be home on time. Do you need a ride to help you get home on time?"

"Mom, you know, the Bible says I've got to obey God before I obey you and I'm studying His Word, so I can stay as late as I want!"

What would you tell Stephanie the next morning?

Case Study 3

For a few weeks now, some of your friends from church have been gathering every Wednesday morning, 20 minutes before school starts, to pray for your school. You think it's a great idea and you'd really like to do it. It's just the kind of stuff that you've been discussing in your youth group.

When you ask your mom to drop you off 20 minutes early for school, she responds, "Honey, if I do that, I have to take your brother to daycare early, and doing that will cost me an extra $20 a month. We just can't afford it."

When your friend calls Tuesday night to ask you if you're going early on Wednesday, what do you say? What do you do?

minutes, then ask each group to get together with another group and share what they wrote about Philippians 3:7-14. After groups have shared their card for that verse, they should switch and share what they wrote about James 1:22-25 with a different group. Groups should continue to switch off until each group has shared both cards two or three times. When everyone is through, re-group and ask, "Was there a theme that stood out in more than one group?"

Explain that obeying God is not always easy, especially if He asks us to do something that our parents or someone else we like or respect might not agree with. A true follower of Jesus is committed to obeying God no matter how difficult it is.

Option 2: Questions of Obedience. For this option, you need your Bible and this book.

1. I'm confused. If I'm supposed to obey God *and* my parents, what do I do when they contradict each other? *Jesus teaches that God should always come first. However, if you think what God wants you to do conflicts with what your parents want you to do, it's best to talk it over with a Christian adult you respect to see if you can come up with a way to obey God and still show respect to your parents.*

2. If God wants us to obey Him over our parents, why do we have to obey our parents at all? *God wants us to obey His commands, but He doesn't want us to ignore our parents. We're supposed to respect and honor them, recognizing that they're the ones God is using to take care of us and teach us about Him.*

3. What if my parents aren't Christians? *If your parents know that you are a Christian, your words and actions can create either a positive or a negative impression on your family about what it means to follow God. If they're seeing Jesus through you and how your relationship with Him affects your attitude toward them, the more they will recognize the powerful difference He makes in your life.*

4. Does being in high school or college make a difference in how I obey God and my parents? *God wants you to obey Him regardless of your age, but the older you get and the more independent from your parents you become, the more you will make your own decisions. This doesn't mean you can stop respecting them and the wisdom that they bring with the years they have ahead of you!*

APPLY

Option 1: Red Light, Green Light. For this option, you need some active students. Ask the group the following questions:

- Why do we have traffic laws and signs? *To make driving safer.*
- What happens when someone disobeys traffic laws? *Tickets, accidents, injuries and deaths.*

Explain that students are going to play a game of Red Light, Green Light to test their driving skills. Here's a quick review of how to play: You are the "Light." Have players line up on one side of the room, opposite from you. Turn your back to the players and yell out "Green light!" This is the cue for players to move as quickly as they can toward you (walking, running, crawling) before you yell "Red light!" and spin around. Anyone caught moving when you turn around must go back to the starting line. Repeat the process several times until someone finally reaches you; then he or she takes your place as the Light and the game begins again.

Play as many rounds as time permits, then explain that usually the people who win this game are the ones who pay close attention and take the smallest steps. They move slowly but steadily, and make their way toward the finish line. Sometimes the same is true with God. When we want to make our way to Him and put Him first in our lives, it's often better to start out with small steps. That way, we don't bite off more than we can chew, only to end up spitting it all out!

Invite students to spend some silent time thinking about one small step they can take this week to put God first, then close in prayer, asking God to help students keep moving toward Him this week, even if at times they feel like they're barely crawling.

Option 2: Showing What It Means to Put God First. For this option, you need some honest students.

Explain that when we place God first before everything else, our behavior should be different from that of others around us. Is that true with you? Ask students to silently reflect on what about them during the past week showed their closest non-Christian friends what it means to put God first in one's life.

Allow a minute or two for quiet reflection, and then invite students to stand who feel they need prayer for doing a better job of showing others what it means to put God first. Take some time to pray for these honest students, asking God to bless them and help them to be incredible witnesses for Him in front of their friends.

REFLECT

The following short devotions are for the students to reflect on and answer during the week. You can make a copy of these pages and distribute to your class or print out from the PDF available online at **www.gospellight.com/ uncommon_jh_parents_and_family.zip**.

1—TWO TRIPS

Check out Matthew 28:18-20. Jesus is talking to you, too!

Imagine this: You signed up to go on a mission trip a few months ago. At first it sounded like it was going to be a lot of fun. After a while though, you started to hear talk about toilet cleaning, sleeping on cement floors and bugs the size of a doorknob in your training meetings. You're starting to get a little nervous about the hard work and yucky conditions, but you have faith that God will help you and your church cope with the conditions and still work well together.

Now imagine that your parents decide to take a fabulous trip to Yosemite, where you have always wanted to go—and it's scheduled for the same week as your mission trip. What would you do?

_____
_____
_____
_____

Are you obedient to God when things get rough? In what ways?

_____
_____
_____

What do you think God wants you to do?

_____
_____
_____

How can you remember to do it God's way before your family's way this week?

_____

_____

_____

_____

_____

2—MEANINGFUL SACRIFICE

Be a good junior-higher and go read 1 Peter 1:14-15!

Pammy had been putting $5 a week into the offering basket at church for a whole year before her mom found out. It was a pretty big sacrifice for her, considering she made $20 a week, if she was lucky, by baby-sitting.

Pammy's mom didn't like the whole "church thing" to begin with, and when she found out, she was really upset with Pammy. "Why are you wasting your money like that?" she demanded. "You should be putting that money in the bank!"

Pammy was really sad and didn't know what to do. She knew that God wanted her to give her money and her mother didn't want her to. She had no idea what she should do.

Obeying God might mean doing things that your family does not approve of. Your family may consider you foolish or weak for obeying God instead of doing what they want you to do. When it comes down to it, who do you obey: God or your family?

Seek counsel from a wise Christian adult and ask God for the strength to follow Him even when it's really, really hard.

3—BAD ADVICE

Read John 13:34-35 and think about love.

There's this kid at school who is being a total jerk, throwing wads of paper and making fun of you in class. You tell your family about it. Whose advice would you take?

❑   Your dad's: "Report that kid to the principal! She should be thrown out of school!"

❏ Your sister's: "You should lay some kind of trap for her so she's the one who's embarrassed! Something involving a garden hose and some Jell-O. Want me to help?"
❏ Your little cousin's: "Push her into a mud puddle or something because she shouldn't treat you like that!"

Do you always do what your family wants you to do, or do you think about what God wants you to do as well?

_____

_____

_____

_____

Whose opinion do you care about more—your family's or God's?

_____

_____

_____

_____

What's one way you can remind yourself today that obeying God comes first?

_____

_____

_____

_____

4—TIME TO TELL

Read Mark 5:1-20. Is it time to tell?

Tim was nervous and happy. He'd been going to church with his friend Alec for a few months, and a couple of weeks ago, he'd become a Christian. Tim was having an amazing time learning about God, going to junior high group and learning how to pray. He felt really close to God and was learning new things every day.

Then Tim began to realize how much his family needed Jesus too, and he began to get nervous—really nervous. What if he told them about Jesus and they laughed at him or told him to shut up? What if they got mad at him and told him he couldn't go to church with Alec anymore?

The more he got to know God, the more Tim saw how much his family needed God and that he was going to have to tell them all the things Jesus had done for him, even though it scared him.

Obeying God can mean sharing things about Him with your family, and that can be scary.

Have you told your family about what God has done for you?

_____
_____
_____
_____

Do you tell them what God can do for them?

_____
_____
_____
_____

Pray that God will give you the courage to be bold and share with those who need to hear about what God has done for you.

A SECOND FAMILY

THE BIG IDEA
Knowing God as your heavenly Father makes you a part of His family.

SESSION AIMS
In this session you will guide students to (1) understand what God's family is like; (2) feel motivated to become an active part of God's family; and (3) choose one way they can help another member of God's family this week.

THE BIGGEST VERSE
"All the believers were together and had everything in common" (Acts 2:44).

OTHER IMPORTANT VERSES
Psalm 133:1-3; Acts 2:42-47; Galatians 6:1; Ephesians 4:11-16; 1 Timothy 2:5

Note: Additional options and worksheets in 8$^1/_2$" x 11" format for this session are available for download at **www.gospellight.com/uncommon_jh_parents_and_family.zip**.

STARTER

Option 1: Miscommunication. For this option, you need just this book.

Greet students and ask for two volunteers to act out the following scenario as it might continue in a typical junior-higher's home (Rachel whines and complains; her mom gets frustrated; Rachel starts to yell; her mom reprimands):

> As Rachel walks through the front door of her house, she finds her mom waiting for her, demanding to know where she's been.
>
> Rachel explains that she was at her friend Nicole's house, and her mom, obviously frustrated, points out that Rachel did not ask permission to go to Nicole's house.
>
> She reminds her mom that she *did* ask permission that morning before she left for school, but Rachel's mom replies that she asked her yesterday, not today. Frustrated by now, herself, Rachel insists that she asked this morning!

Allow five minutes or so for the performance, then ask for two new volunteers to act out the same scenario as it should happen if Rachel and her mom are both trying to demonstrate Christ's love.

When they have finished the scene, discuss:

- Which is most like your own family?
- Which is most like most families you know?
- What was different in the two scenarios?
- Is it realistic to think we can always show Christ's love to others in our family?

Transition to the rest of the session by explaining that we can't be perfect in the way we love our family, but as we'll see today, once we know Jesus, we become part of God's family—and knowing God and being part of His family should make a difference in how we act toward our earthly family.

Option 2: Picturing the Perfect Family. For this option, you need several adult volunteers, 3x5-inch index cards, pens or pencils, a whiteboard, a dry-erase marker and a stopwatch.

Greet students and divide them by gender, then distribute eight index cards and a pen or pencil to each team. Direct teams to opposite sides of the room where their conversation won't be overheard (or have one team go outside the room with an adult volunteer to supervise) and instruct the teams to write one quality of a "perfect" family on each of the eight index cards. Some suggestions include *fun, caring, honest, sharing.*

Allow five minutes for brainstorming, then ask for a volunteer from the guys' team to come forward and choose one of the index cards from the girls' team. When you give the signal, you will start the stopwatch and the volunteer must use the whiteboard to draw a picture that represents what is on the card—he cannot speak or use numbers in his picture. His teammates will attempt to identify the quality written on the card as fast as they can. The adult volunteers should stand around the group to listen for someone to guess correctly. Once the guys' team identifies the quality, stop the watch and record the time, and then repeat the process with the girls' team. After all cards have been identified, congratulate the team with the lowest overall time score, then discuss:

- Is there such a thing as a perfect family? Why or why not?
- What about God's family? Is it perfect?

Explain that today you're going to discover a lot more about being part of God's family and how we can help it to be as great as possible!

MESSAGE

Option 1: *Pleasantville*. For this option, you need several Bibles, a TV, a DVD player and the film *Pleasantville*. (*Note*: this film is rated PG-13, so be sure to pay attention to any objectionable language or content as you show this carefully selected scene to your students.)

Ahead of time, cue the video approximately four minutes from the opening graphic to the scene in which the boy overhears his mom on the phone talking to his dad. The mom and dad are fighting because both of them want to go out and have fun, and neither of them wants to be responsible for taking care of the kids.

Play the clip, and then discuss:

- How should parents feel about being around their kids? *They should feel good about spending time with their kids.*
- How would you feel if you found out that your parents didn't want to be around you? *Rejected, angry, hurt, unloved, and so forth.*

Explain, "Guess what? Not one of us has a perfect family here on earth. We all get sick of each other at times. But the Bible describes a group of people who acted like a family and really seemed to enjoy each other." Read Acts 2:42-47. Point out that this was the first church that formed after Jesus was resurrected. It's important to note that the people didn't just sit around and tell stories or jokes; they spent time teaching each other. When they broke bread, they not only ate together but also celebrated Communion together. Just as Jesus and His apostles shared everything, the Early Church continued this practice and its people pooled all of their money. As they continued to praise God, nonbelievers saw that there was something special about this group of people and the God they served, causing the nonbelievers to want to join them.[1]

After you've given the students background on the Early Church, discuss:

- If there was a teenager in *this* story from Acts, what might he overhear his mom and dad say? *"Honey, let's hang out with our kids!"*
- How would he would feel? *Secure, happy, loved, content, and so on.*

Explain that it's natural at times to feel frustrated with our own family. The good news is that we're members not just of our immediate family, but when we come to know Jesus as Savior, we become part of God's family too.

Option 2: Learn, Share, Praise, Grow. For this option, you need candy bars for everyone. Ahead of time, ask a student or adult volunteer to share about what he or she has been learning about God. Also ahead of time, divide the amount of the candy in half so that it will look like you don't have enough for everyone.

Read Acts 2:42-47, then explain that this passage describes how the early believers lived after Jesus was resurrected and ascended to heaven.

1. *They learned (Acts 2:42).* Invite the volunteer to come forward and share what he or she has prepared, then offer that it's pretty encouraging to hear what others have been learning about God, isn't it? The Early Church spent a lot of time telling each other what they were learning and the things God was teaching them.

2. *They shared with others (Acts 2:44-45).* Before you introduce this point, explain that you have some candy bars, but not enough for everyone. Distribute the candy to about half of the students and let them know that it's okay to eat them. Allow time for a couple bites;

then stop them and ask for a show of hands: "How many of you decided to share what you had received with someone else? How many of you even *thought* about sharing what you had?"

Explain that members of the Early Church shared everything. They were expected to. In fact, they were so used to sharing that they didn't even have to think about it; it was just something they did. Hand out the rest of the candy.

3. *They praised God (Acts 2:47)*. Explain that it's easier to praise God than we think. We don't have to jump around and sing all the time. There are all sorts of other ways we can praise Him. One way is Alphabet Praise. Explain how this works: Beginning with the letter A, and going through the alphabet, you say a word that describes God, such as "awesome" or "amazing."

Lead students through the Alphabet Praise (you'll have to get creative for some, like "x-cellent" and "zebra maker" or "zippy"); then explain that the next time you're feeling bored or sad, try thinking of letters in the alphabet and qualities of God that match those letters and you're sure to feel better before long!

4. *They grew (Acts 2:47)*. Ask students to indicate the number of people in their immediate family by holding up that number of fingers. Explain that there are several ways that a family can get bigger, including the birth of a baby, marriage and adopting a child. Explain that in God's family, there's only *one* way to add someone: that person needs to ask Jesus to become Savior and Lord over his or her life. *That's* what happened to the first Christian church. Nonbelievers saw that the believers were different, and they wanted to be a part of that wonderful fellowship.

Youth Leader Tip

Many of your junior-highers will come from fragmented families. Home, for some of them, can be an unhappy (and even dangerous) place. Be prepared for students' reactions by carefully considering what you know about your students, and be sensitive to their needs.

DIG

Option 1: God's Family. For this option, you need several Bibles, 3x5-inch index cards, felt-tip pens, one or two copies of "God's Family" (found on the next page), several adult volunteers and pens or pencils.

Ahead of time, give a copy of the handout and four index cards each to several volunteers from the church congregation. Ask them to read the passages listed on the handout and record their personal understanding of each passage on a separate index card. What does it mean for them in everyday life, when it comes to being a part of God's family? (Ask them to write the Scripture reference on the back of each card for ease in sorting them later.) Collect the cards from your volunteers a day or two before your group's meeting. (*Note:* Asking people in your congregation isn't just handy for this activity—it's intended to give students a picture of how others in their own church feel about being a part of God's family.)

Also ahead of time, sort the cards by Scripture reference, creating four groups; then place each group in a separate area of the meeting room (no need to hide them). Use an index card and a felt-tip pen to write the Scripture reference for each group, and attach the card somewhere above the stack of cards so students will know which passage to look up.

Explain that you've asked several people to write their opinions about the Church on index cards. Distribute Bibles and divide students into pairs, then point out the four areas where you've placed the cards. Instruct students to look up the Scripture reference in each area and read the responses on the index cards.

Allow enough time for students to finish each of the four stations, then have everyone regroup and ask each pair to share which person's reaction they agreed with the most. Then ask, "What things did you learn about being a part of God's family from these passages?"

Explain that there's a lot more to being a part of God's family than just getting together for meals and holidays. We have to learn to love each other and how to deal with each other's differences. We've all got different abilities and gifts that God wants us to use to serve each other and His kingdom.

Option 2: Less Than Ideal. For this option, you will just need the following case study.

Explain that being part of God's family is a wonderful thing! Unfortunately, sometimes those of us in His family don't treat each other very well. Share the following:

GOD'S FAMILY

PSALM 133:1-3	EPHESIANS 4:11-16
GALATIANS 6:1	I THESSALONIANS 5:12-13

Using an index card to record your answers, please apply the following two questions to each of the Scripture references listed above:

    What does this passage say about being a part of God's family?

②   How might you put this into practice in your church?

My name is Jessica and I've been going to church most of my life. When I was in fourth and fifth grade, it was pretty fun. All of my church friends went to my school, and we always had a lot of fun together at school and at church.

In sixth grade, everything changed. My friends and I were going to different schools and we only saw each other at church.

When we're at church, all my friends talk about are people they know from their school—and I don't know any of them. I feel totally left out. I've tried talking to them about it, and they said they would try to include me more, but that only worked for about five minutes. Pretty soon they were talking about some food fight at lunch and how great it was when the fire bell rang during a huge algebra test. Boy, church sure isn't like it used to be anymore.

Ask for volunteers to read the following Scripture verses: Psalm 133:1-3; Galatians 6:1; Ephesians 4:11-16; and 1 Thessalonians 5:12-13, pausing between each to discuss how this could be lived out in an ideal church, and how it seems to be lived out in reality. Discuss the following:

- What advice might you give Jessica? *You might want to advise Jessica not to rely on her time at church as the only time she spends with her friends. She could call them during the week and keep in touch so she doesn't feel like a stranger.*

- What advice might Jessica's pastor give her? *Pray for her friends and ask that God would provide ways for her to reach out to them. She could also reach out to newer members of her church and invite them to meet with her and her friends. The great part about this is that not only will Jessica be acting as a true member of God's family by reaching out to others, but the new people will also bring a different dynamic to the group and everyone can have a chance to get reacquainted.*

- How should the people in God's family treat each other? *They should be caring and compassionate.*

Conclude by saying that being part of God's family means that we're supposed to be considerate and love each other. This means staying on the lookout for the "Jessicas" in our lives and reaching out to them.

APPLY

Option 1: Working with the Family. For this option, you need paper and felt-tip pens. (*Note:* If you know you have students who have not taken the steps to be part of God's family yet, take time to invite them to do so in this step!)

Explain that when we asked Jesus to be our Savior, we became part of the wonderful family we learned about today. Let's consider where each of us might fit in the family of God.

Distribute paper and felt-tip pens and ask students to draw pictures (faces, symbols, figures) representing different people they know in the church. Next to each picture, have them write some of the things that person does in the church. (For example, students might write "encourages" next to a friend's picture or "teaches" next to a picture of an adult leader.) Then instruct students to draw a picture of themselves and a few things that they could do (or already do) in the church. When all the students have finished, invite them to share their pictures.

Explain to students that serving in your church could be as simple as making a point to introduce yourself each time you see a newcomer, volunteering an hour per week helping out in the nursery or picking up trash on the church grounds. Whenever you give of yourself and help others in the church, it is important work as a member of God's family.

End in prayer, thanking God for the opportunity to serve others in His family and asking Him to show students ways that He wants them to serve. Have a few moments of reflection, encouraging students to pray silently and allow God to speak to their hearts to show them how they can show His love to others.

Option 2: Praying for Each Other. For this option, you will just need an adult volunteer.

Explain that one of the great things about being part of God's family is that we can be real with others who know Him. We can share what's going on in our lives and how we need His help.

Set a tone of vulnerability by sharing a prayer need that you have and allowing the adult volunteer to pray for that need. Then invite students to share, one at a time, something tough going on in their lives that they need prayer for. As each person shares, another student should volunteer to pray for him or her. Continue until all prayer requests have been addressed, then close in prayer, thanking God that He has given us the support and love of other family members and asking Him to help students to share His love and support with others in the coming week.

REFLECT

The following short devotions are for the students to reflect on and answer during the week. You can make a copy of these pages and distribute to your class or print out from the PDF available online at **www.gospellight.com/ uncommon_jh_parents_and_family.zip**.

1—JUST LIKE FAMILY

Hey there, buddy—slow down and read 1 Timothy 5:1-2!

Imagine that you're at church camp and you've just finished an awesome time of group worship and prayer. Now everyone is having a good time relaxing around the blazing fire in the center of your circle. What might someone think who just happens by and doesn't know anything about your group?

- ❑ A bunch of teenagers are up to no good. Those young folks are always making trouble.
- ❑ Are those some type of Scouts? What in the world are they doing? Are they makin' s'mores? I wonder if they'd make one for me.
- ❑ What a great family to hang out together like that!

Guess what? When God looks at you and other Christians gathered together, He sees a family. That's right—brothers and sisters in His kingdom. Do you treat other Christians as part of your family or just as random people that don't matter very much to you? Explain.

_____

_____

_____

_____

_____

What's one way you can show a sister or brother in Christ that you think of him or her like one of your family today?

_____

_____

_____

_____

2—A NEW FAMILY

Go check out the lost and found in Mark 10:29-30.

After months of her father asking her to come live with him, Teresa decided to take him up on his offer and move from New Mexico to Wyoming. It was a really hard decision for her to make, as leaving New Mexico meant leaving her mother and her three brothers, all of her friends, and the church she loved.

In Wyoming, Teresa would have to go to a strange new school and make new friends. Not only that, but her father didn't believe in Jesus like she and her mom did, and she was afraid that he wouldn't let her go to church. However, Teresa really loved her dad and wanted him to know Jesus. In fact, she wanted it so much for him that she was willing to move to help her dad get to know Him.

When Teresa got to Wyoming, she really missed her mom and brothers. Her dad was fun and he was happy to have her there, but she felt like she didn't really have the family she needed anymore. It wasn't until she found a church and other Christians to talk to and depend on that she felt at home and started enjoying her life with her dad.

God provides families for us in many ways. Sometimes it's our actual family, but God also uses the people in our churches as a new family.

Thank God today for your flesh-and-blood family and for your other family—the brothers and sisters and mothers and fathers you have in the family of God.

3—FAMILY TIME

Hey, sister! Hey, brother! Go read Mark 3:31-34 right now!

Who do you hang out with most of the time? Don't worry, you can pick more than one!

- ❑ Preppy kids with nice wardrobes
- ❑ Skaters and punks who listen to cool music
- ❑ Smart kids who get straight *As*
- ❑ Just the most popular people
- ❑ Student-government people
- ❑ People who try to do what God wants them to do

Do you think the kind of people you hang out with affects the type of person *you* are?

_____

_____

_____

_____

_____

_____

Do you serve God better because of your friends?

_____

_____

_____

_____

_____

Do you think God wants you to hang out with just anybody, or with your brothers and sisters in His family?

_____

_____

_____

_____

_____

Evaluate your friends in prayer today and ask God if you need more time with your family in Christ.

4—EVERYBODY NEEDS SOMEBODY

Pull up a chair and find Psalm 68:4-6.

Garrett was a pretty happy-go-lucky guy with lots of friends and a great family who was always around to help him figure out what life was all about. Then, last fall, everything changed.

First, Garrett's older sister moved thousands of miles away to go to college, and then his older brother got married and moved to Tokyo. To top it all off, his dad was laid off from his job. It wasn't long before Dad got another job, but the new one was hundreds of miles from the town where Garrett had grown up.

In the new town, Garrett's parents didn't have much time for him because of their new jobs and trying to get their new house in order. Garrett felt really alone without his siblings, his old friends and his parents. He prayed and prayed for God to fill the holes in his need for family as he looked for a new church.

God doesn't want His children to be lonely. That's why He sets up families for us, not only your actual family but also people in His Church.

Are you lonely? Pray that God will provide family members—other believers—you can depend on when life is hard and who will celebrate with you when life is great.

HOW TO RESOLVE CONFLICTS WITH FAMILY MEMBERS

Conflict in families is nothing new; in fact, it is a common theme in many stories in the Bible. One example of such family strife is the story of Jacob and his brother, Esau, told in Genesis 27–33. What's interesting about this story is not just the drama that occurs between Jacob and Esau, but also the way in which Jacob finally approaches his brother to resolve the conflict. In so doing, he provides us with a clear method for how we can approach a family member with whom we are experiencing conflict to work out a resolution.

The main issue that sparked the brothers' conflict began when the boys were adolescents. One day, Jacob, the younger brother, was cooking some stew. His older brother, Esau, had just come into the camp from a hunting trip, and he was famished. He asked Jacob for some food, and Jacob agreed on the condition that Esau gave up his birthright (see Genesis 25:29-34). Later, Jacob deceived their aging father, Isaac, into giving him a final blessing that was intended for Esau (see Genesis 27:18-40).

Esau was understandably upset with his brother, and he vowed to take revenge (see Genesis 27:41). Jacob, fearing for his life, fled from his brother and took refuge with his uncle. After many years had passed, God told Jacob to go back to the land of his fathers (see Genesis 31:3). So Jacob began to prepare to make the return trip—and to prepare to finally face his brother.

The story of their meeting is told in Genesis 32:1-20 and Genesis 33:1-12. Notice in this passage that there are several important steps that Jacob took to resolve the conflict with his brother.

1. *Jacob identified the problem and admitted his fears.* "Save me, I pray, from the hand of my brother Esau, for I am afraid he will come and attack me" (Genesis 32:11).

2. *Jacob took initiative in resolving the conflict.* "Jacob sent messengers ahead of him to his brother. . . . He instructed them: 'This is what you are to say to my master Esau. . . "I am sending this message to my lord, that I may find favor in your eyes" ' " (Genesis 32:3-5).

3. *Jacob prayed about the problem.* "Then Jacob prayed, 'O God of my father Abraham . . . save me, I pray, from the hand of my brother' " (Genesis 32:9,11).

4. *Jacob put himself in his brother's shoes and tried to anticipate his resistance.* "For he thought, 'I will pacify him with these gifts I am sending on ahead; later, when I see him, perhaps he will receive me' " (Genesis 32:20).

5. *When Jacob met Esau, he communicated how he felt.* "[Jacob] himself went on ahead and bowed down to the ground seven times as he approached his brother" (Genesis 33:3).

6. *Jacob took action to correct the problem (he made restitution).* "If I have found favor in your eyes, accept this gift from me. For to see your face is like seeing the face of God, now that you have received me favorably. Please accept the present that was brought to you, for God has been gracious to me and I have all I need" (Genesis 33:10-11).[1]

Hopefully, you will never face a conflict with a family member as drastic as the one Jacob faced with his brother, Esau. However, even in situations in which the slightest misunderstanding has occurred, you can use these steps to get to the heart of the issue and resolve the matter before it gets worse. When you follow these steps and approach conflicts with family in love, God will reward your efforts and help you to work through these issues.

UNIT II
Family & Friends

"The hardest place to follow Jesus is at your home."

This was one of the constant refrains of Mike, my own youth pastor as a teenager. Part of why I still remember this theme in Mike's teaching was because at the time, I thought he was right. Now that I'm an adult—and a parent—I'm even more convinced.

So how can we help our teenagers show the love of Jesus in their own homes? How can we help them treat their family members like they would like to be treated?

Remember Your Own Struggles as a Teenager

When I was in high school, I hated emptying the dishwasher. When my mom would tell my brother and me that we had to empty the dishwasher, we'd argue over which of us would clear the top rack and which of us would empty the bottom. Emptying either rack took us a total of about 45 seconds, but we'd spend five minutes fighting before we even got started.

I also hated bringing in the groceries when my mom returned from the store. When her car pulled in the driveway, I'd run up the stairs of our two-story home, hoping that my mom wouldn't bother to call my name and make me come down the stairs. That strategy never worked. My mom would summon me and make me come downstairs and empty the groceries.

In both cases, I spent more time avoiding the task than it actually took to do the task. And, by the way, I was a student leader at church. At church, I was happy to volunteer to help my youth leaders clean out the youth kitchen and haul in luggage from the retreat. But I dreaded comparable chores at home.

What were your own struggles at home as a teenager? Beyond the simple chores I've described above, what were your greatest sources of conflict? How did the way your parents treated you make you feel about yourself? How did you feel about the way your parents acted when you had friends over? The more you remember those situations, the more you'll be in touch with your students' experiences and struggles today.

Share the Ways You're Trying to Love Your Family

All of us are on journeys of growth and transformation—including you. How much are you sharing with your students about your efforts to love your family—including your parents—these days?

Have you told them about the surprise date you planned for your spouse?

Do they know about your special birthday ritual with your kid?

Whether or not you're married, do they know about the flowers you sent your mom or step-mom on Mother's Day?

None of us is perfect, but odds are good that even the small ways you love your family will make an impact on your youth ministry.

I still believe home is the hardest place to be a Christian. But hopefully your openness and your teaching will make it at least a little bit easier for your students.

Kara Powell
Executive Director of the Fuller Youth Institute
Assistant Professor of Youth, Family and Culture
Fuller Theological Seminary

STICKS AND STONES

THE BIG IDEA

Family members and friends don't speak negatively about each other; they encourage one another.

SESSION AIMS

In this session you will guide students to (1) understand the consequences of negative speech; (2) feel challenged to become encouragers; and (3) commit to careful and purposeful speech this week.

THE BIGGEST VERSE

"Brothers, do not slander one another. Anyone who speaks against his brother or judges him speaks against the law and judges it. When you judge the law, you are not keeping it, but sitting in judgment on it" (James 4:11).

OTHER IMPORTANT VERSES

Proverbs 12:18; Matthew 12:34-35; John 15:20; Acts 17:1-15; James 4:3-12

Note: Additional options and worksheets in 8$^1/_2$" x 11" format for this session are available for download at **www.gospellight.com/uncommon_jh_parents_and_family.zip**.

STARTER

Option 1: Important Words. For this option, you need talkative junior-highers (man, oh man, where can you dig up some of those?).

Greet your students and ask them to form three groups (or more if you have more than 30 students). Tell students that they are about to conduct a language experiment and that each group will only be able to use certain types of speech. Assign one group to speak without using the words "the," "a" or "an." The second group cannot use the words "me," "my" and "I." The third group may speak only in questions. Instruct students that they'll have four minutes to mingle and try to have a short conversation with at least one person from each group.

When four minutes have passed, discuss the following:

- How did you feel during our experiment?
- Which group had the easiest time conversing? Why?
- Was it hard to be conscious of the way in which you spoke? Why or why not?
- How much attention do you normally pay to the things that you say? Explain.

Conclude by explaining to the group that how we speak plays a very important role in our relationships with our family and with others. It can make or break a relationship in a matter of seconds. Today, as we discuss how God wants us to treat our friends and family, we are going to start by looking at our words.

Option 2: Positive and Negative. For this option, you need an episode of a popular TV show that features family relationships (and a way to show it to your group) and paper or pens. Ahead of time, record an episode or locate one on the Internet. Choose a 2 to 4 minute inoffensive clip that contains a lot of dialogue between at least two family members.

Youth Leader Tip

A common misconception about Christianity held by non-believers and believers alike is that it consists of a list of do's and don'ts. As you teach the lessons in this book, remember to emphasize that students need to be in relationship with Jesus in order to be God-pleasing friends.

Greet students and explain as you are distributing paper and pens that you have a TV clip that you're going to play. Ask everyone on the left side of the room to note the things the characters say that could be considered negative (such as put-downs, gossip or accusations). Have those on the right side write down anything said or done that is positive or encouraging. Play the clip once or twice as time allows so that students can make adequate notes.

Discuss the students' observations about the TV characters' speech by asking each group to share what it recorded that was positive and negative. At the conclusion, ask the group what they noticed about the way these characters spoke that they would say is similar to things they have heard in their family. What was different? Ask them whether they agree or disagree with this statement: *Family members never speak negatively about each other.*

Conclude by explaining the way we speak to people makes a big difference in the kind of relationships we have with them. Today, as we discuss how God wants us to treat our family, it makes sense to start with a lesson on language.

MESSAGE

Option 1: *Hook*. For this option, you need Bibles, a copy of the film *Hook*, a TV and a DVD player. Ahead of time, cue the video to the scene where Peter and the boys sit down to an imaginary meal (approximately one hour and 11 minutes from the opening TriStar Pictures graphic). The scene lasts about four minutes, ending with Peter flicking imaginary food on Rufio's face.

Distribute Bibles and ask students to turn to Acts 17:1-15. Allow each willing junior-higher to read a verse until they've read the whole passage. Show the movie clip, and then discuss:

- Why do you think Peter hesitated to respond to Rufio in the way Rufio expected? *Peter was a polite adult businessman, and they don't typically call each other the kinds of names Rufio called Peter (at least not out loud and in public).*

- Do you think Peter felt pressured to call Rufio names? Why or why not? *Definitely. The other Lost Boys cheered for Rufio and booed Peter. But Peter probably also felt internal pressure to act in what he felt would be an appropriate manner.*

- How were the Jews in Thessalonica like Rufio? *Both caused a scene as they spewed negative speech about an undeserving person.*

- What do you think would have happened if Paul had responded to the Jews the way Peter eventually responded to Rufio? *Paul might have landed in jail and few would have heard or accepted the saving message of Jesus.*

- Is it fun to put others down? Explain. *It can be, but it's seldom fun to be the one on the receiving end.*

Ask someone to read Proverbs 12:18 and then ask students:

- How does this verse apply to the scene from *Hook*? *Peter caved to the pressure and turned out to be better at the name-calling game than Rufio, but Rufio and their relationship got hurt in the process.*

- How about to Acts 17? *Scripture doesn't say, but it's likely Paul was hurt by the Jews rejection of him and his message about Jesus. Paul intended to bring true healing with his words; the Jews' reckless words cut them off from their chances to receive that healing.*

- Do you think the Lost Boys respected Peter more or less at the end of the scene? *They appear to respect him more, but Rufio sulks off by himself and apparently doesn't share their respect for Peter.*

- How could Peter have acted differently? *He could have held his ground and not given in to Rufio's name-calling. He could have chosen to encourage the obviously insecure Rufio.*

- Is it ever a sign of weakness to choose encouragement over a comeback? Why or why not? *No, it's actually a sign of courage and strength to resist the easy response of a comeback and go for the more uncommon and difficult response of encouragement.*

Option 2: Prickly Marshmallows. For this option, you need Bibles, large marshmallows and toothpicks.

Distribute Bibles and ask for five readers to read three verses each of Acts 17:1-15 while others follow along. When the passage has been read, instruct students to pair up and give each pair a marshmallow and at least six toothpicks. Tell pairs to insert the toothpicks all around the marshmallow, then have students form two lines so that pairs face one another and can just touch each other's fingertips. Designate one line to start with the marshmallow, tossing it under-handed to their partner. Those that successfully complete the toss take one step back and their partner will toss it back to them. Continue this process until you have a winning pair.

When the game is completed, have everyone sit down, and then explain that in many ways, the game we just played is like our words and the impact they have on our family and others—they can be painful. Ask, "In the passage we just read, who had negative speech spoken about them? How do you think they felt? How do you think it felt for your partner to catch the marshmallow? How is that like being the person about whom others speak badly?"

Explain that negative speech hurts others. In this story, Paul, Silas and Jason were hurt when others said negative things about them. When we choose to throw bad words around, either to or about someone else, we make the choice to hurt others.

But get this: Not only do negative words hurt others, but they also hurt us. Ask, "How did it feel to throw your marshmallow? How might speaking negatively hurt the one who has spoken it? Who in this passage spoke negatively? What did they say?"

Explain that the Jews got hurt when they spoke negatively about Paul and Jason. Their rush to prevent Paul's preaching meant that they didn't take time to listen. They missed out on the opportunity to understand and believe in Jesus as the Christ. When you choose to throw bad words around, you also end up hurting yourself.

Next, allow the junior-highers to remove toothpicks and split the marshmallow with their partner so that everyone has one-half marshmallow to eat. Explain that encouragement tastes sweet. The Bereans not only encouraged Paul by their eagerness to hear the message of Jesus, but they in turn gave Paul a chance to encourage them as they accepted the message as truth.

Ask for a volunteer to read Proverbs 22:11 and explain that just like the toothpicks pricked your hands no matter whether you were catching or throwing, the way you speak can hurt you, your family and others. Or you can choose to be an encourager, which benefits you and everyone around you—like sharing your sweet-tasting marshmallow with your partner.

DIG

Option 1: Taste Test. You will need a jalapeno pepper, a bag of individually wrapped chocolates, copies of "Taste Test" (found on the next page) and pens.

Hold up the jalapeno and ask for a show of hands of those who would like to eat it. Take a count (if you need to!) and choose a volunteer to eat the

Taste Test

Circle the food that you would rather eat regularly.

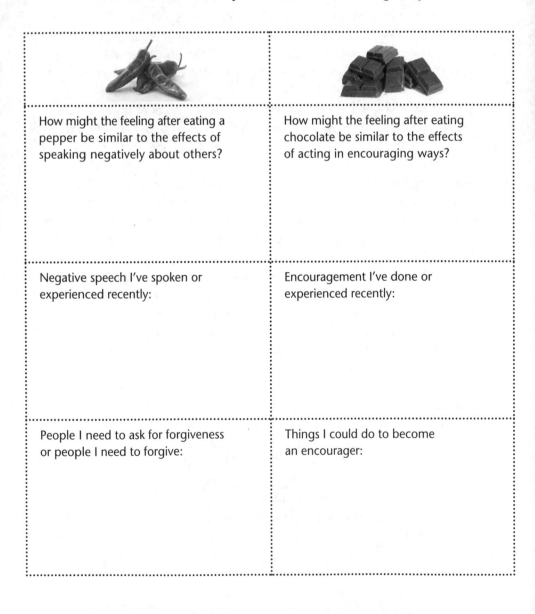

How might the feeling after eating a pepper be similar to the effects of speaking negatively about others?	How might the feeling after eating chocolate be similar to the effects of acting in encouraging ways?
Negative speech I've spoken or experienced recently:	Encouragement I've done or experienced recently:
People I need to ask for forgiveness or people I need to forgive:	Things I could do to become an encourager:

pepper. Ask your volunteer to describe how his or her mouth feels after eating the pepper. (*Note:* You may want to have a slice of bread or a glass of milk on hand to help stop the burning.)

Next, hold up a chocolate and ask for a show of hands of those who would like to eat it (don't show junior-highers that you have more than one). Count hands, and then allow a volunteer to eat the chocolate and describe how his or her mouth feels after doing so.

Pass out the "Taste Test" handouts and allow a few minutes for students to complete them. Discuss why so many more students wanted to eat the chocolate rather than the pepper. (A few students will probably choose the pepper, some because they genuinely like peppers and others just to be contrary or to stand out. And very likely some do prefer negative speech to encouragement. It's okay. Allow your kids to be honest.) Ask students to share their answers to the first question in each column on the handout, and then discuss:

- Which would you prefer to experience regularly: the effects of negative speech or encouragement?
- Why does it sometimes seem so hard to be an encourager, especially to those who know us best: our family?
- What do we have to lose by being more encouraging? What do we have to gain?
- What could you do this week to be more encouraging to your family and to others?

Give everyone a chocolate, reminding them of the sweetness of encouraging words as you transition to the final step of the lesson.

Option 2: Which Ending? For this option, you need this book and some honest junior-highers. Read the following story to your students:

Nick and Rick, who were twin brothers, studied together for their science test. They prepared study cards from their textbooks and quizzed each other on what they thought would be important information to know for the test. Both boys thought they did okay, but when their teacher returned the exams, Nick scored an *A*, whereas Rick got a *B*.

Divide students down the middle, so that half are sitting on the left of the room and half on the right. Explain that when you point to the left side of the room, you want students to raise their hands with a suggestion for something Rick could say or do that would be negative or hurtful to Nick. When you point to the right side, you want a show of hands with suggestions for something Rick could say or do that would be positive or encouraging to Nick.

Point to the left side and hear one of their answers. Then, point to the right side for one of their responses. Continue going back and forth, getting suggestions for negative and positive things to say or do.

Then ask students which ending they would choose if they were in Rick's position. Which ending would they want Rick to choose if they were Nick? If students have different answers for those two questions, ask why. You could also vote to see which answer is most likely for both of the above two questions; then for those two options, discuss what Rick had to gain and lose by following that option.

APPLY

Option 1: Examples. For this option, you need copies of "Examples" (found on the next page) and pens or pencils.

Ask students to form pairs as you pass out pens or pencils and the "Examples" handout to each person. Instruct junior-highers to read 1 Timothy 4:12-13, then reflect on the verses as they read and respond to each situation. Remind them that they want to specifically avoid negative speech and look for ways to be an encourager in each situation.

After a few minutes, instruct pairs to join with another pair and share some of their favorite answers (if pairs didn't have time to address each situation, the other pair can offer their suggestions). Give groups another few minutes to talk it over.

Bring students back into a larger group and discuss:

- How does being an example in speech affect the other areas in which Christians should serve as examples?
- How does using negative speech affect our Christian example?
- What does verse 13 mean when it says "devote"?
- In what practical ways can we do that?
- How would doing so affect our speech and our Christian example?

Ask junior-highers to write on the bottom of their handouts a similar situation that they expect to face this week, either with their family or their friends.

EXAMPLES

Don't let anyone look down on you because you are young, but set an example
for the believers in speech, in life, in love, in faith and in purity. Until I come,
devote yourself to the public reading of Scripture, to preaching and to teaching.
1 Timothy 4:12-13

Your brother makes fun of your new haircut. You . . .

_____

_____

The fast-food clerk is obviously rude to you. You . . .

_____

_____

You overhear your mom tell your grandma that she wishes you got good grades like your sister. You . . .

_____

_____

A deacon at church says he doesn't think junior-highers are mature enough to serve as ushers. You . . .

_____

_____

Your sports team plans a car wash fundraiser for a Sunday morning. When you suggest it could be on a Saturday instead so that you can attend church on Sunday, a teammate says church is for losers. You . . .

_____

_____

A similar situation that you expect to face this week . . .

_____

_____

_____

_____

Then ask them to create a response in which they avoid negative speech and act as an encourager. Close in prayer, asking God to strengthen students' resolve to live as Christian examples in their speech.

Option 2: I'm Prepared. For this option, you need Bibles, copies of "I'm Prepared" (found on the next page) and pens or pencils.

Ask students to sit in a circle and think of (not say) the following two things: (1) an emotion such as sympathy, delight or frustration, and (2) a simple silly sentence such as "I like toothpaste." Allow a few moments for students to think, and then ask them to whisper the emotion to the person on their right and the sentence to the person on their left. Remind students to remember what their neighbors have said to them.

Explain that one by one, the students will say the statement whispered to them by the person on their left using the emotion whispered to them by the person on their right. (*Example:* "I like toothpaste!" said in anger.)

When everyone has had a turn, explain that the way each sentence was spoken made a difference in how the group perceived the sentence. If someone growled at us that they liked toothpaste, we would probably doubt just how much they liked toothpaste (at least their particular brand).

Ask for a volunteer to read 1 Peter 3:15-16 while others follow along. Ask, "Do you think it would be possible for someone to use negative speech as they try to share about Jesus? If so, how?" Explain that there are inappropriate ways to share the gospel. If someone sounded judgmental while sharing about Jesus' love, it wouldn't make sense. The listener might be more likely to reject the gospel as they reject the speaker. The gospel needs to be shared with gentleness and respect.

But like Paul, who shared the gospel using good reasoning, explanations and proofs (see Acts 17:2-3), even if we share the gospel appropriately, we might become the target of negative speech. Because of that, we might be tempted to avoid talking about Jesus in order to avoid ridicule. However, the

Youth Leader Tip
Words hurt. But that can be hard to admit, especially if you are an insecure adolescent. As a youth leader, it's your job to provide a safe environment where students can be themselves and feel accepted for who they are.

Paul went to the synagogue. Places I go where people might be ready to hear about Jesus:

_____

_____

_____

_____

_____

Some Jews believed in Jesus. People I know who might be ready to believe in Jesus:

_____

_____

_____

_____

_____

Paul said that the Christ had to suffer and rise from the dead, and that Jesus was the Christ. I could say:

_____

_____

_____

_____

_____

encouraging thing to do in these situations is to point people to the truth rather than allowing them to believe lies.

Pass out copies of "I'm Prepared" and pens or pencils to each student. Explain that the handout is based on Acts 17:1-15, then allow a few minutes for students to complete the statements. In response to the third statement, encourage students to think of their own testimony as a way to share about Jesus with others. When junior-highers have finished, ask for a few to share what they might say to others about Jesus (you might prod a little note-taking so they gain from others' good ideas).

Ask students to close their eyes and listen prayerfully as you read 1 Peter 3:15-16 again. Ask students to quietly commit to God to encourage at least one other person by sharing the gospel. After a few moments, pray that students will be gentle as they explain the reason for their hope and that God will bless their efforts in His name.

REFLECT

The following short devotions are for the students to reflect on and answer during the week. You can make a copy of these pages and distribute to your class or print out from the PDF available online at **www.gospellight.com/ uncommon_jh_parents_and_family.zip**.

1—WRONG WAY TO FEEL BETTER

Take a minute to read 1 Thessalonians 5:11. Now do what it says!

Dante had a secret: He really admired his older brother. Damien was so good at everything he did, including schoolwork, basketball and guitar, and everybody thought he was cool (including Dante—though he would never tell Damien that!).

The problem was that Damien was so busy with all of his activities and friends that Dante might as well have been invisible. Damien mostly ignored him. Dante very badly wanted his brother's attention, and it seemed like the only way he could get it was to be annoying and insulting.

Dante called Damien "Lame-ien" to his face and behind his back. He barged uninvited into the garage when Damien practiced with his band, Easy Does It. He rolled his eyes and muttered "What*ever*" when anyone complimented Damien's successes.

What should Dante do instead? (You can check more than one!)

❏ Let Damien know that he would like to watch Easy Does It practice (because they are awesome!), but that he will wait to be invited
❏ Change Damien's nickname from "Lame-ien" to "He-Got-Game-ien"
❏ Just ignore his brother from now on and try not to care
❏ Apologize for being bratty and let his older brother and others know how proud he is to be Damien's little bro

Sometimes we say and do negative things because we're insecure—*not* because the other person deserves it. Think about a time during the past week when you said something negative to or about a family member or friend. Did you say it to make yourself feel better?

Spend a minute or two in prayer today, asking God to help you show His love to your family and friends. You might be surprised how good you feel when you do what's right!

2—DON'T GET SNAPPY

Get wise and memorize Proverbs 12:16!

Lila hated it when her dad called her his "Chubby Bunny." That had been his name for her for as long as she could remember, and she knew he didn't mean it as an insult . . . but it still hurt her feelings. Lila was a little pudgy and they both knew it, but did Dad have to rub it in?

One afternoon after a really hard day at school, Lila dragged herself through the front door of her house. "Dad, I'm home!" she called.

Dad came out of his office. "How's my Chubby Bunny?" he asked, giving her a hug.

Lila pushed him away and screamed, "I hate you!" and then ran upstairs to her room.

With Proverbs 12:16 in mind, what might have been a better way for Lila to handle her frustration with her dad?

_____

_____

_____

_____

_____

Think about a time during the last month when you overreacted to something that a family member said to you. Did your quick response make the situation better or worse?

_____

_____

_____

_____

_____

How might the situation have turned out differently if you had taken time to think about your words before you said them?

_____

_____

_____

_____

Before you snap a reply to a friend or family member's hurtful words, try to breathe deeply, count to 10 and say a quick prayer. Time is on your side!

3—FIERY TONGUES

Avoid a catastrophe! Read Proverbs 21:23.

After Jesus' crucifixion, resurrection and ascension, His disciples followed His instructions and waited. They weren't sure exactly what they were waiting for, but when it happened, it was obvious to everyone that *this* was what Jesus had promised:

> When the day of Pentecost came, they were all together in one place. Suddenly a sound like the blowing of a violent wind came from heaven and filled the whole house where they were sitting. They saw what seemed to be tongues of fire that separated and came to rest on each of them. All of them were filled with the Holy Spirit and began to speak in other tongues as the Spirit enabled them (Acts 2:1-4).

After all you have learned about the importance of our words, do you think it's significant that the Holy Spirit appeared to the first disciples as fiery tongues? Why or why not?

_____

_____

_____

_____

_____

_____

The Holy Spirit is available to every person who believes in Jesus as Savior. If you desire the Spirit's power to control your words, write a short prayer below, asking Him to fill you just as He filled Jesus' first disciples. He may not appear as tongues of fire, but His presence will guide and change you—for real!

_____

_____

_____

_____

4—QUICK-SLOW-SLOW

Quick! Check out James 1:19-20.

Jesus' brother James, who was a very important leader in the Early Church, wrote this formula for godly relationships:

Everyone should be *quick* to listen, *slow* to speak and *slow* to become angry (James 1:19, emphasis added).

When you're *quick* to listen, you learn a lot about your family and friends. Maybe your sister is sad or frustrated and needs someone to talk to. Maybe your grandma needs help and is embarrassed to come right out and ask. How will you know if you don't take time to listen?

When you're *slow* to speak, you give yourself time to think (and even pray!) about your words before you say them. You are more likely to say exactly what you mean in a kind and respectful way, instead of popping off and regretting it!

When you're *slow* to become angry, you save yourself and everyone else a lot of headaches. Anger is not always a bad thing—when people or circumstances aren't fair to you or those you love, anger is understandable! (Read Ephesians 4:26,29-32 for instructions on how to deal with your anger appropriately.) Most of the time, however, frustrating or hurtful situations are best handled with calm and kindness rather than anger. If you take a breath and talk it through with your family member or friend, you're likely to work it out without getting steamed.

Write yourself a "QUICK-SLOW-SLOW" reminder and put it up in a spot where you'll see it. After a couple of days following the formula, do you notice a difference?

KEEPING THE PEACE

THE BIG IDEA

Family members and friends don't provoke one another; they try to get along peacefully.

SESSION AIMS

In this session, you will guide students to (1) learn what it means to provoke others; (2) feel responsible for their role in developing peaceful relationships; and (3) pledge to become a peacemaker this week.

THE BIGGEST VERSE

"Let us not become conceited, provoking and envying each other" (Galatians 5:26).

OTHER IMPORTANT VERSES

Judges 13:1-6; Psalm 37:32-34; Proverbs 13:10; Matthew 5:23-24; James 3:17-18

Note: Additional options and worksheets in 8^1/$_2$" x 11" format for this session are available for download at **www.gospellight.com/uncommon_jh_parents_and_family.zip**.

STARTER

Option 1: Provocative Beginnings. For this option, you need not a thing!

As students arrive, whisper one of the following instructions to every third student:

- Stare at people
- Tickle people
- Stand in people's personal space
- Defensively say, "What's it to you?"
- Say, "I can do that!" to anyone who does something
- Do something to bug others

Allow students to hang out for a few minutes and interact with each other as they carry out your instructions in secret.

Gather the group and then discuss:

- What unusual behavior did you notice from some people today? How did their actions make you feel? Explain.
- Those of you who received instructions, how did you feel about doing what was asked? How did others respond to you? Did that make you want to continue or stop following my instructions? Explain.

Tell students that your instructions were intended to provoke responses from others. Ask students what they think it means to provoke (*to try to get a reaction from someone, generally by doing something annoying or troublesome*). Ask the following:

- How do you deal with it when others purposely try to get a reaction from you?
- How often during a day do you think you either provoke someone yourself or feel provoked by others?
- How different do you think your life might be if you tried to not provoke others?
- What is an alternative to provoking people?

Explain that even though provoking responses from people can be a common (and sometimes very funny!) way to relate to people, family members and friends should try to get along peacefully. As we'll see today, provoking one another is one of the "one anothers" that we're *not* supposed to do to each other.

Option 2: *Tommy Boy*. For this option, you need a copy of the movie *Tommy Boy*, a TV and a DVD player. (*Note:* This film is rated PG-13 and has some scenes that may not be appropriate for junior-highers. Do yourself, your senior pastor and your students' parents a favor and show only the clip recommended for this option!)

Ahead of time, cue the video to about 49 minutes from the opening Paramount Pictures graphic, beginning with scenery footage of the car sailing down the road. Cut the scene after just less than three minutes when Richard climbs out of the car.

Greet students and ask them how many have been on a long car trip with their family. Ask how many got in a fight with a sibling and had their parents yell at them from the front seat. Ask, "What caused those fights? Why does it seem so impossible to have a peaceful road trip?"

Tell junior-highers that you're going to show a video of another exhausting and anything-but-peaceful road trip. Play the scene from *Tommy Boy*, and then discuss:

- What caused Tommy and Richard to fight? *Richard provoked this fight by insulting Tommy.*

- How could they have avoided the fight? *Richard could have chosen not to provoke Tommy; Tommy could have chosen not to rise to the bait.*

- How do junior-highers provoke each other?

- If you had been riding in the car, what could you have done to promote a peaceful relationship?

Explain that it's all too easy to give in to the temptation to provoke others, or try to get a reaction from them, generally by doing something annoying. This is especially true if our patience has been taxed, as on a car trip. But as we'll see today, God has something else in mind.[1]

MESSAGE

Option 1: Paper Fight. For this option, you need Bibles, three copies of the "Samson and Delilah Skit" (found on the next two pages), stacks of old newspapers, masking tape, a whistle and a stopwatch.

Ask girls to group on one side of the room and guys to gather on the other side. Give each group a large stack of newspapers and tell them they have one

SAMSON AND DELILAH
Adapted from Judges 16:4–21

Narrator: Samson fell in love with a woman named Delilah. The Philistine rulers said to her, "See if you can lure him into showing you the secret of his great strength and how we can overpower him so we may tie him up and subdue him. We will pay you a fortune."

> **Ask:** *"What would you do if you were Delilah? Why?"*

Delilah: Samson, tell me the secret of your great strength and how you can be tied up and subdued.*

> **Ask:** *"Does Delilah's response surprise you? Why or why not?*
> *If you were Samson, how would you respond to Delilah? Why?"*

Samson: If anyone ties me with seven fresh cords that have not been dried, I'll become weak as any other man.*

Narrator: The Philistine rulers brought seven fresh cords to Delilah, and she tied Samson with them. With men hidden in the room, Delilah called out . . .

Delilah: Samson, the Philistines are upon you!

Narrator: But Samson snapped the cords like string too near a fire and the secret of his strength was not discovered.

> **Ask:** *"Does Samson's response surprise you? Why or why not?*
> *If you were Samson, how do you think you would have felt during this scene?*
> *Explain. If you were Delilah, how do you think you would have responded*
> *when you realized Samson had lied to you?"*

Delilah: You have made a fool of me; you lied to me. Come now, tell me how you can be tied.*

Samson: If anyone ties me securely with new ropes that have never been used, I'll become as weak as any other man.*

Narrator: So Delilah took new ropes and tied him with them. Then, with men hidden in the room, she called out . . .

Delilah: Samson, the Philistines are upon you!*

Narrator: But Samson snapped the ropes like thread.

> **Ask:** *"Why do you think Samson played along with Delilah? Why didn't*
> *he just ditch her, since she obviously wanted to hurt him?"*

Delilah: Until now, you have been making a fool of me and have been lying to me. Tell me how you can be tied.*

Samson: If you weave the braids of my head into the fabric on the loom and tighten it with the pin, I'll become weak as any other man.

Narrator: So, while he was sleeping, Delilah did just that. Again she called out . . .

Delilah: Samson, the Philistines are upon you!*

Narrator: But Samson pulled up the pin and the loom with the fabric.

Delilah: How can you say, "I love you," when you won't confide in me? This is the third time you have made a fool of me and haven't told me the secret of your great strength.*

Narrator: With such nagging, she prodded him day after day until he was tired to death.

> ***Ask:*** *"What do you think of Samson and Delilah's friendship?*
> *How do they provoke each other? At this point, what would you*
> *do if you were Delilah? If you were Samson?"*

Narrator: So Sampson told her everything.

Samson: No razor has ever been used on my head because I have been a Nazirite set apart to God since birth. If my head were shaved, my strength would leave me, and I would become as weak as any other man.

Narrator: Delilah saw that Samson had told her everything and sent to the Philistine rulers to come back. They returned with the money. Delilah put Samson to sleep on her lap and called a man to cut off his hair. And his strength left him.

Delilah: Samson, the Philistines are upon you!*

Samson: I'll go out as before and shake myself free.

Narrator: Samson did not know that his strength and the Lord had left him. Then the Philistines seized him, gouged out his eyes and took him away in shackles to prison.

> ***Ask:*** *"Why did Samson finally give in? How do you think Delilah*
> *felt when they took Samson away? Do you think she had really*
> *thought through the consequences to her actions? Explain."*

minute to make paper balls. While they work, tape a line down the middle of the room. After one minute, take away any remaining stacked newspaper.

Ask for three readers to read the roles of Narrator, Samson and Delilah. Give volunteers the scripts and ask them to stand with you at the front of the room. Tell students that the volunteers will read them a story in which two Bible characters provoke each other. You might need to remind students about the definition of provoke: "to try to get a response from someone, usually by being annoying or mean."

When Delilah provokes Samson, the girls will have 10 seconds to throw paper balls at the guys. When Samson provokes Delilah, the guys will have 10 seconds to throw paper balls at the girls. Paper can only be thrown on your cue and must stop when you blow the whistle. Only those throwing the paper can touch paper during those 10 seconds.

Advise readers to pause where they see an asterisk. For every asterisk, give the cue for either girls or guys to throw their paper, depending on whether Samson or Delilah read that line.

(*Note:* If you are copying the scripts in this book to hand out to your students, also advise them to disregard the questions in italics in their scripts. The student scripts available for download do not contain these questions.) After the reading, discuss the following:

- How is provoking someone like throwing something at them?

- What do you think of Samson and Delilah's relationship? How did they provoke each other?

- Girls, if you had been Delilah, would you have handled this situation differently? If so, how?

- Guys, if you had been Samson, would you have handled this situation differently? If so, how?

Youth Leader Tip

As you discuss the story of Samson and Delilah, be sure to emphasize to students that if Samson's internal life had been devoted to God, he wouldn't have had a relationship with Delilah in the first place.

Ask a volunteer to read Galatians 5:26, and then ask:

- Which characters in the story of Samson and Delilah showed signs of being conceited?
- Who envied whom?
- How could this story have been different if one or both of them had chosen not to provoke the other but to try to get along peacefully?

Ask students why they think some people act conceited. Why do they provoke others? Why are they envious? As you ask these questions, make sure you point out that many of these behaviors and attitudes are motivated by insecurity and envy. Although people who are envious, conceited and provoke others seem to be quite confident, in general their actions flow from their lack of confidence.

Option 2: Samson and Delilah Skit. For this option, you need Bibles and three copies of the "Samson and Delilah Skit" (found on pages 120-121).

Ask students to sit in a circle. Explain to the group that Samson was a judge of Israel, which meant he served as a governor. His authority included military, judicial, and spiritual responsibility for Israel. Before he was born, an angel appeared to his mother and told her that Samson would be a "Nazirite." A Nazirite man observed certain acts of purity, including no drinking, eating only "clean" food, and never cutting his hair (see Judges 13:1-6). Most Nazirites took vows lasting only for a set period of time. At the completion of their vows, they offered special sacrifices, including the cutting and burning of their hair.

Samson himself may not have understood the secret of his strength. The Nazirite's external signs were intended to represent the inward life devoted to God. If Samson had had that kind of relationship with God, he would not have had a relationship with Delilah in the first place. Samson seems to have put more faith in God's gift of his strength than he put in God.[2]

Next, assign one girl to read the part of Delilah and one boy to read the part of Samson, and ask them to sit in the center of the circle. Choose volunteers who will really ham it up. Read the part of the Narrator yourself, and then discuss the questions as they are placed in the copy of the script in this guide. (*Note:* the student scripts available for download do not contain these questions. If you are copying the scripts in this book to hand out to your students, advise them to disregard the questions in italics in their scripts.)

After the reading, ask for a volunteer to read Psalm 37:32-34 and then ask students how this Scripture applies to Samson and Delilah. How could this story have been different if one or both of them had chosen not to provoke the other but to try to get along peacefully?

DIG

Option 1: Relationship Seesaw. For this option, you need a Bible, a TV and a video camera. Ahead of time, grab a few of your junior-highers, go to a nearby playground and film them playing on a seesaw for 4-5 minutes. If you have time, edit the footage together with background music; if not, plan to just show the raw video.

At the meeting, ask students to describe their favorite playground activity as children and what they enjoyed about that activity. Explain that you took a few of the students to reenact what used to be one of your favorite activities. At this point, play a minute or two of the video, and then lead the following discussion while the video is still playing in the background. (If it becomes too distracting, you can turn if off and just lead the discussion.)

- How might a relationship be like a seesaw? *Two people need to agree to be on the seesaw (or relationship) and they have to work together to make it work.*

- So who has responsibility for making the seesaw (or the relationship) work? *Both people.*

- In a relationship, what might it look like to "sow in peace" (James 3:18)? *Listen to your family members and friends, do nice things for them, encourage them when they need it, be available to spend time together, and so on.*

- What kind of "harvest of righteousness" could a peacemaker reap in a good relationship? *A family who gets along and doesn't fight; a good, solid friend (or perhaps lots of them), and the peace of mind that you've been a good son or daughter, brother or sister, and friend.*

Explain that just like two children on a seesaw need to be about the same size, two people in a relationship need to put in about the same amount of effort. It's cause-and-effect: If you put in the effort, the other person will probably put in as much effort. If you try to get along peacefully, the other person probably will, too. But if you provoke them, they might provoke you right back. If you take responsibility to be a peacemaker, you'll probably have peaceful relationships. Even if members of your family or your friends sometimes try to provoke you, you can have the peace that comes with trying to do what is right.

Option 2: Foul! For this option, you need nothing but this book.
Read the following case study to your students:

> Marcus is an eighth grader on his school's basketball team. He is a pretty good player, but is lousy at free throws. One Friday, his team was playing their big rivals and Marcus was doing really well. He had scored 18 points in the first half alone.
>
> At the start of the third quarter, the guy guarding him started slapping and pushing him, especially when the referee wasn't looking. At first, Marcus thought it was maybe just an accident, but when the guard kept doing it, he knew it was intentional. He was intentionally trying to throw Marcus off his game.

- What should Marcus do?
- If Marcus wanted to avoid being provoked, what should he do?
- Have you ever been in a situation like Marcus? If so, what did you do? Looking back, what would you have done differently?

APPLY

Option 1: Target: Peace. For this option, you need a Bible, copies of "Target: Peace" (found on the next page) and pens or pencils.

Read Proverbs 13:10 and explain that when we think too much of ourselves, it's easy to provoke others. That way, we feel better than others because we had the power to make them look stupid or feel angry. But if you take the Bible's advice and avoid provoking others, your relationships will be strengthened *and* you'll feel better about yourself.

Distribute the handouts and pens or pencils and give students a few minutes to think through when they feel like provokers and how they can become peacemakers. Ask if anyone is willing to share what he or she will do to become a peacemaker (remind students not to share too specifically—you don't want a spontaneous gossip session!). Close in prayer, asking the Spirit to work in students' hearts to make them wise peacemakers.

TARGET: PEACE

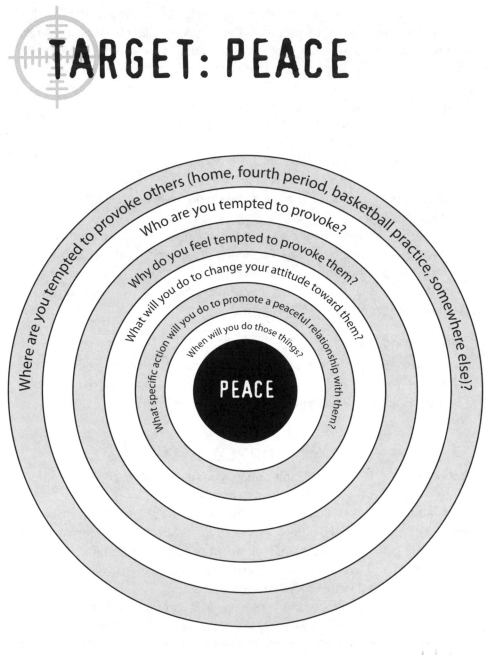

Where are you tempted to provoke others (home, fourth period, basketball practice, somewhere else)?

Who are you tempted to provoke?

Why do you feel tempted to provoke them?

What will you do to change your attitude toward them?

What specific action will you do to promote a peaceful relationship with them?

When will you do those things?

PEACE

Option 2: Heart of Peace. For this option, you need Bibles, colored construction paper, scissors and markers.

Explain that Jesus was the ultimate Peacemaker, bringing together a holy and loving God with a sinful world. However, while He intended to point people to His Father, the truth of His message offended many who rejected Him. As we live out our faith before people, we too will be rejected—just because we love Jesus.

Ask for a volunteer to read John 16:33, and then ask:

- What does this verse tell you about your relationship to the world? To Jesus?
- How do you think Jesus wants His followers to respond to the world that gives them trouble?

Explain that the world *will* provoke Jesus' followers. Maybe the students have already felt provoked because they are Christians. But they don't have to get angry or provoke others in return. They can have peace and spread peace because Jesus is in control.

Instruct students to either cut out or draw a heart on the construction paper. Tell them that as Christians and peacemakers, they can offer peace to others as they share about Jesus. Ask students to pray silently over their heart, asking God with whom He wants them to share His message of peace. Invite them to write the name or initials of one person, then fold the heart and keep it somewhere they will be reminded to pray for that person until God provides a time and opportunity for them to share about Jesus.

Youth Leader Tip

Unless you're discussing sensitive material and you would prefer to have students in groups with good friends, use creative means to mix students up. For example, you could pass out a Lifesaver candy to each student and then have them form groups based on its color.

REFLECT

The following short devotions are for the students to reflect on and answer during the week. You can make a copy of these pages and distribute to your class or print out from the PDF available online at **www.gospellight.com/ uncommon_jh_parents_and_family.zip**.

1—PEACE IS NOT OPTIONAL

Check out Ecclesiastes 7:9, and check your spirit too.

When someone tries to provoke you—to get a reaction out of you by being insulting or annoying—you've got a few options. Check each option below that you have done in the past:

- ❑ Insulted the person right back
- ❑ Lashed out physically by pushing, hitting, kicking or pinching
- ❑ Gossiped about the person to others
- ❑ Decided never to speak to the person ever again

Now make a short list of options you can choose from if you are serious about being a peacemaker.

_____

_____

_____

_____

Share your list with a family member and a friend who will help keep you accountable to your decision, and ask God for His Spirit to guide you.

2—KEEPERS AND MAKERS

Keep up by reading Matthew 5:9. Whose son or daughter are you?

Watching or reading the news, you may have come across the words "peacekeeper" or "peacekeeping mission" in an article about an overseas conflict. Or maybe you've heard your local police called "keepers of the peace."

Peace*keepers* are usually present in an already-peaceful situation to make sure everyone follows the law and meets their obligations to society.

Peace*makers*, on the other hand, sometimes have an even more difficult job: to bring peace and stability where none exists. Peacemakers courageously risk being insulted, rejected or—in some cases where violence has broken out—even injured or killed in order to bring harmony and reconciliation between people. Peacemaking is a tough job, and it's understandable why not many people apply for it!

Here's the surprising part: As tough as being a peacemaker is, every single one of Jesus' followers is called to be one! The apostle Paul wrote that God "reconciled us to himself through Christ and gave us the ministry of reconciliation" (2 Corinthians 5:18).

Wherever we go, our goal should be to bring peace between people and to share with them how they can also have peace with God (by trusting His Son, Jesus).

Are you ready to become a peacemaker? Spend a few minutes in prayer today, asking your Father in heaven to show you what you can do to bring peace to hurting people around you.

3—WHAT ALL THE (KIND) KIDS ARE WEARING

There are a few items of clothing that never go out of style. Read about 'em in Colossians 3:12.

Tana's little sister drives her crazy! Five-year-old Mia loves to sneak into Tana's closet to play "big-girl" dress-up. Apparently Mia has good fashion sense, because she always picks Tana's favorite clothes—the clothes Tana saves up her babysitting money to buy!

This morning, Mia "borrowed" a brand-new sweater that Tana had only worn once. And then she spilled grape juice on it! The sweater is ruined. Check each box next to an action that would provoke Mia in return (yep, there's more than one):

- ❑ "Borrow" Mia's most-loved teddy bear, Donnie, and "accidentally" spill grape juice on him
- ❑ Make a Big-Girl Dress-Up Box for Mia and stock it with clothes Tana doesn't want anymore—and keep the good clothes out of reach
- ❑ Hold Mia down and pull her hair, and maybe give her a hard pinch for good measure

❑ Make a "Do Not Enter" sign and booby-trap her door to catch Mia in the act

The fourth option *might* not provoke Mia (she really should stay out of Tana's room unless she's invited), but it doesn't pass the Colossians 3:12 test. Circle the option above that passes with flying colors.

A little kindness goes a long way toward keeping the peace. How will you be kind today?

4—DOWNWARD SPIRAL

What did the apostle Peter say about insults? So glad you asked! Find out in 1 Peter 3:9.

Here's something you may already know about trading insults: If it goes on for very long, it's bound to get nasty. One of Jesus' apostles, Peter, warned against getting sucked in by the downward spiral. Fill in the blanks below:

Do not repay evil with _____ or insult with _____, but with _____, because to this you were called so that you may inherit a blessing (1 Peter 3:9).

Did you catch that last part? You will be blessed when you choose to bless others instead of slamming them!

In Matthew 5:9, which you looked at earlier in the week, Jesus says that peace-makers are blessed because "they will be called sons [or daughters] of God." What does it mean to you to be called God's son or daughter?

_____

_____

_____

_____

Now think of a time someone insulted you. What is one way you could have shared the blessing of being God's child instead of repaying insult with insult?

_____

_____

_____

_____

THE TRUTH, AND NOTHING BUT

THE BIG IDEA
Family members and friends don't lie; they speak the truth in love.

SESSION AIMS
In this session you will guide students to (1) learn that no lie is little or white; (2) feel compelled to honest and loving speech; and (3) give God control of their tongues by choosing one specific new way to act this week.

THE BIGGEST VERSE
"Therefore each of you must put off falsehood and speak truthfully to his neighbor, for we are all members of one body" (Ephesians 4:25).

OTHER IMPORTANT VERSES
Exodus 20:16; Proverbs 12:22; Matthew 25:45; James 3:8-10; 1 Peter 5:8

Note: Additional options and worksheets in 8¹/₂" x 11" format for this session are available for download at **www.gospellight.com/uncommon_jh_parents_and_family.zip**.

STARTER

Option 1: *Liar, Liar.* For this option, you need a copy of the film *Liar, Liar,* a TV and DVD player. (*Note*: this film also has PG-13 rating, so be sure to pay attention to any objectionable language or content as you show this carefully selected scene to your students.)

Ahead of time, cue the video to about $38\frac{1}{2}$ minutes from the opening Universal graphic, beginning with Max's dad borrowing him from class. The scene lasts about three and a half minutes until recess is over and Max returns to class.

At the meeting, greet students and play the clip. Then discuss:

- Do you agree with Max's dad that you have to lie to get along in the world? Why or why not?
- What do you think about the lie Max's dad told his wife when she was pregnant?
- When do you feel most tempted to lie?
- Would it be hard to go an entire day without lying? Explain.
- What value does our culture place on truthfulness? Do you think you value truthfulness more or less than our culture? Explain.

Explain that just like we saw in the clip, we are all tempted to lie to one another. But as we'll see today, God has something different—and far better—in mind!

Option 2: Who's Telling the Truth? For this option, you need three or six student volunteers (depending on how many rounds you decide to play), paper and pens or pencils. (Depending on your time, the number of students you expect to attend and the amount of interesting and obscure knowledge you have about students, you can choose to play one or two rounds of the game.)

Ahead of time, choose one or two students about whom you know something interesting that others probably don't know (you may need to make a few calls to get some good info). For example, perhaps a student spent a year in Germany at age five, or a student knows how to juggle. You'll also need to prepare two other students to pretend that information is true about them. Choose students who can act convincingly. Also, choose facts that won't be immediately obvious (saying that one of them spent last Christmas in Germany when two of the three went to last year's winter retreat is not a good choice).

At the meeting, greet students and then ask your volunteers to stand with you at the front of the room as students form three teams. Tell students that it's their job to figure out which one of your volunteers is telling the truth (hence, the name of the game). Each of the volunteers will answer questions as if something is true about themselves, but only one will be telling the truth.

Then name the specific fact (for example, "One of these guys got shoved into the girl's bathroom at school"). Distribute paper and pens and allow teams a minute to brainstorm a list of questions they would like to ask the volunteers.

Beginning with the team with the youngest member, allow each team to choose two of the volunteers to answer the same question from their list. After that team asks one question, the next team does the same thing, then the third team, then the first team again, and so on. Teams should pay attention both to the questions asked and volunteers' responses in order to wisely choose the questions they ask next—and to guess which volunteer is telling the truth.

You can choose whether to allow each team a certain number of questions or whether to play for a set amount of time. Either way, at the end, give teams one minute to confer about who they think is telling the truth.

As you point to each volunteer, ask teams to vote by cheering enthusiastically for the volunteer they chose. Finally, ask the volunteer who's telling the truth to step forward. Now discuss the following:

- What did the impostors do that made you want to believe them?
- How difficult was it to tell the lies from the truth? Explain.
- On a scale of 1 to 10, with 10 being high, how good were the impostors at lying?
- On a scale of 1 to 10, how good are you at lying?
- How often do you think you tell a lie?
- Why do people lie?
- Is lying helpful or harmful? Explain.

Let's face it: We are all surrounded by lies and are tempted to do it ourselves. But, as we'll see today, God has something different—and far better—in mind!

Youth Leader Tip
It might be easier to coordinate this activity and less obvious if you have three adult leaders or church members who are familiar to the students participate as volunteers.

MESSAGE

Option 1: Truth Relay. For this option, you need Bibles and lots of obviously old clothing items (funky hats, shirts, shoes, socks, and the like. Try a thrift or army surplus store).

Form two even teams and send them to opposite ends of the room. Instruct each team to split in half and form single-file lines facing each other across their end of the room. Then give each student one to three items of old clothing to put on (depending on how many items you have), preferably items that don't fit them well. (Clothing should be put on over their regular clothes.)

Tell students that, on your signal, the first person on one side of the room will run to their teammate, take off their items of clothing, say something truthful and positive about that person to their face (for example, "Your hair looks nice today," "You're a good soccer player," "I appreciate that you help me with my math homework"). At that point, the person who has just heard something truthful about themselves should put that clothing on (in addition to the items they are already wearing) and then run across the room to the next person in line to repeat the process. As the relay goes down the line, players will have to put on and take off more and more items of clothing. The first team done wins. Consider rewarding the winners with their pick of the old clothes.

Invite students to open their Bibles to Ephesians 4:25, and then ask:

- How does this verse apply to our game? *We had to take off something that didn't fit, tell the truth and work together as a team.*

- If someone had chosen not to say something truthful to their teammate and instead lied, how might that have affected your team? *It might not have had a big effect if nobody noticed. But if the rule breaker was caught, the team could have been disqualified.*

- How is that like what happens when someone lies? *Sometimes people get away with lies. But sometimes it causes big problems, like people not being able to trust each other. Even if they get away with it, lying can bring on guilt and other emotional problems and get in the way of their relationship with God and each other.*

- How much faster would this game have been if you didn't have to take something off? How might falsehood slow down relationships?

Explain that there are two alternatives to taking off falsehood: leaving it on or never putting it on in the first place. Explain that falsehood—or lying—is like a cancer that you choose to allow to invade your relationships. Just like cancer cells multiply and spread, eating away at a body, one lie leads to another and eats away at relationships. When you choose to lie, you choose to have sick relationships.

Option 2: Stand Up, Sit Down. For this option, you need Bibles, a whiteboard and a whiteboard marker.

Have students form small groups of four to six with others who share their preference for either cookie dough or chocolate brownie ice cream (yes, they have to choose between only two—kinda like choosing between deceit and honesty). Ask groups to open their Bibles and read Acts 4:34–5:11. While they read, write the following questions on the whiteboard for groups to discuss:

- What was Ananias and Sapphira's lie?
- To whom did Ananias and Sapphira lie?
- Why was their lie such a big deal?

After a few minutes for small-group discussion, gather students' attention. Explain that you will read a series of statements. If they think the statement is true, they should stand. If the statement appears to be false, they should sit. Some of these statements are tricky, so they should choose carefully. In between each statement, ask one or two students why they are standing or sitting and what makes that statement true or false.

- No one in the Acts church wanted for anything. *False. The church, through property sales, took care of people's needs, not necessarily all their desires. We can be almost certain that some members of the church would have wanted a new sporty chariot with gold-rimmed wheels, but that doesn't mean they got it!*
- Ananias and Sapphira had to sell their property. *False. Ananias and Sapphira chose to sell their property.*
- Ananias and Sapphira could have kept all the money from the property sale. *True. The money was at their disposal (see 5:4).*
- When Ananias and Sapphira lied to the apostles, they lied to the Holy Spirit. *True (see 5:3-4). Our sins against other Christians are sins against God (see also Matthew 25:45; Acts 9:1-5; and 1 Corinthians 8:12).*
- Ananias and Sapphira lied because they had done something wrong. *False. The lie was their "something wrong."*

- Ananias and Sapphira could have given however much they wanted to give as an acceptable offering. *True. If they hadn't misrepresented the money as the total sale price, the offering would have been acceptable. God cares more about our hearts than the exact amount that we give.*
- Ananias and Sapphira wanted to appear more generous than they were. *True. They lied to win favor with the church.*
- People in this church shrugged off this incident as no big deal. *False. Great fear seized them and likely caused them to be more careful about how they lived (see 5:5,11).*
- The moral of this story is "Don't lie to church officials." *False. The point is "Don't lie to anyone." Period.*
- According to this story, God takes dishonesty seriously. *True! He allowed two people to die as a result of their lies.*

Explain that Ananias and Sapphira lied to make themselves look more generous than they were. Keeping the money wasn't the problem; the money was theirs to keep. But God allowed Peter to see through their lie, and He took it seriously as something that could divide the church if allowed to go unnoticed. In fact, God took it so seriously that He allowed Ananias and Sapphira to die. If only Ananias and Sapphira had presented the money for what it was, they could have avoided the tragic ending to their story.[1]

DIG

Option 1: The Parable of Truth and Falsehood. For this option, you need Bibles and this book. Read the following story:

Once upon a time, Truth and Falsehood met each other on the road.
    Falsehood asked, "How are you doing these days?"
    "Not very well at all," sighed Truth.
    Falsehood glanced at Truth's ragged clothes. "You look like you haven't had a bite to eat in quite some time."
    "To be honest, I haven't," admitted Truth. "No one seems to want to employ me nowadays."
    "Come with me, and I'll show you how to get along. . . . But you must promise not to say a word against me while we're together."
    So Truth promised and went along with Falsehood because he was so hungry. Falsehood at once led the way to the very best table at the very best restaurant.

"Waiter, bring us your choicest meats and sweetest sweets!" he called, and they ate and drank all afternoon. When they could hold no more, Falsehood called for the manager.

"I gave that waiter a gold piece nearly an hour ago, and he still hasn't brought our change."

The manager summoned the waiter, who said he'd never even seen a penny out of the gentleman.

"What?" Falsehood shouted. "I can't believe this place! Innocent, law-abiding citizens come in to eat, and you rob them of their hard-earned money! You're a pack of thieves and liars. You will never see me again!"

The manager, fearing that his restaurant's reputation would suffer, brought Falsehood change for the gold piece he claimed to have spent. Then he took the waiter aside and called him a scoundrel, and said he had a mind to fire him.

On the street, Falsehood gave a hearty laugh. "You see how the world works?"

"I'd rather starve than live as you do," Truth said.

And so Truth and Falsehood went their separate ways.[2]

When you finish the story, discuss:

- How did Falsehood's lies affect others?
- Do you agree that Truth has fallen on hard times? Why or why not?
- Do you agree with Falsehood that this is how the world works? Why or why not?
- Falsehood got away with his lie, but did he really benefit from it?
- Imagine Truth and Falsehood are real people. Do you think they can have a friendship? Why or why not?
- If you played the role of Truth, how would you deal with someone like Falsehood?

Ask for two volunteers and assign one to read Exodus 20:16 and the other to read Romans 13:10. Explain that Exodus 20:16 is one of the Ten Commandments, and therefore part of the Law referred to in Romans 13:10. Ask, "Why is it loving to be honest?" (*Love doesn't hurt others. Lying does.*)

Ask students if they can think of a situation in which it would be loving to lie. Allow a few students to share, and then ask the class to help them think of loving and truthful alternatives to lying. (The key here is to show that even "white" lies or "harmless" lies can be avoided.)

To get even more tangible, you might want to ask about some of the following scenarios that students often use as justifications for lying:

- If a person asks if you like their new haircut and you don't, what could you do or say instead of lie? *You could focus on what you do like about it, such as that their bangs look nice.*

- What about if someone asks what you think about the new kid in your history class, and you think he is kind of dorky? *Again, focus on elements of the truth that you can share, such as that he seems nice, but that you don't really know him very well yet.*

Explain that you can almost always find a truthful alternative to lying. If you can't, you'd be better off not saying anything. Just as Truth decided to part ways from Falsehood, you may find it hard to keep important relationships if you lie.

Option 2: "Larry-Boy! And the Fib from Outer Space!" For this option, you need a copy of the *Veggie Tales* episode "Larry-Boy! And the Fib from Outer Space!"; a TV, a DVD player and a Bible.

Ahead of time, cue the episode to the scene about six minutes from the opening Big Idea graphic, which begins with Laura saying the tea party is almost ready. The scene lasts about three minutes, until Junior says, "Well . . ."

Show the clip, and then ask:

- If you were Junior, what would you do? Why? *Lie so that you don't get in trouble; tell the truth, because even if you lie the truth will eventually come out and you'll get in trouble anyway.*

Youth Leader Tip

Young adolescents are just beginning to look outside of their own situations to the needs of others. You have the amazing God-given opportunity to walk with your students as they enter a new life stage.

- What do you think of the way Laura handled the situation? *I would have left, too. She lied to Junior, because she didn't really have to go. She could have stayed and helped Junior.*
- How might a lie affect Junior's relationship with his dad? *What his dad doesn't know won't hurt him, but Junior will know that he lied, and that might hurt their relationship; when his dad finds out, he'll be hurt not only because Junior broke his plate but also by Junior's deception.*
- If Junior blames Laura for breaking the plate, how could that affect his friendship with her? *Laura suggested that they find another plate, which would have avoided the problem. She'll be angry.*
- What do you think might happen if Junior tells the truth? *He might get in trouble. Or his dad might understand that accidents happen. Telling the truth now could avoid a lot of problems.*
- Is there such a thing as a "fibrilius minimus" or a little lie? *Maybe there's such a thing, but I have yet to meet a lie that stays little; most lies lead to more lies, and can quickly get out of control.*

Read Ephesians 4:25, and then ask:

- If Junior knew this verse, how might it help him? *It says not to lie but to tell the truth. It could have helped him realize that he is connected to his dad and to Laura like parts of one body.*

- How would applying this verse to this situation help his relationships with others? *Just like a finger doesn't want to hurt an eye, members of the same body shouldn't hurt each other by lying to one another.*

Explain that one reason people lie is that they get themselves into trouble that could have been avoided. Another reason is that they don't want to admit they've made bad decisions—they want to appear better than they are. Either way, lies hurt relationships. If Junior chooses to lie now, the truth will still come out in the end.

APPLY

Option 1: The Game of Truth Telling. For this option, you need "Truth Telling" cards and game boards (see the sample on the next page; the actual cards and game board can be downloaded at www.gospellight.com/uncommon_jh_ parents_ and_family.zip), pens or pencils, dice, colored game pieces and a Bible.

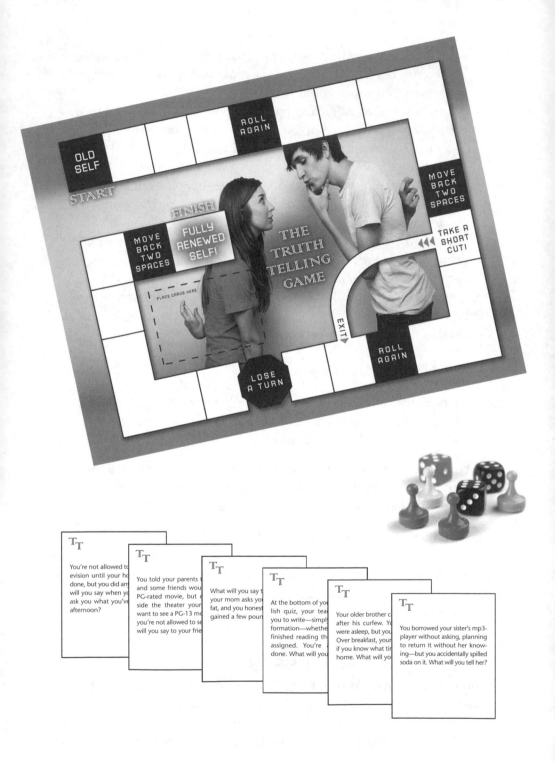

Ahead of time, copy and cut out a set of "Truth Telling" cards and a game board for every four students. (These will work best printed on cardstock, if possible.) You can use pieces from any board game so long as you have one for every student. (If you don't have game pieces, you can give each student in the four-person group a different-colored square of construction paper.)

At the meeting, ask students to form groups of four as you distribute the game-playing supplies as well as pens or pencils. As you do, ask for a volunteer to read Colossians 3:9-10, then explain that even after we begin a relationship with Jesus, we need to keep putting off the old sinful self and putting on the new self. We make choices that allow God to work in us to make us more like Him. The beginning of the game board represents the old self. Your game piece represents your new self today. The end of the game board represents your new self fully renewed in knowledge and in God's image.

Explain that choices to put off the old self involve more than not lying, but for the purposes of the lesson this game focuses on lying versus truth-telling.

Begin by asking each student to fill in one blank Truth Telling card with a hypothetical situation in which he or she would be tempted to lie. Once they're done, ask them to shuffle the cards and stack them face down next to the game board. Tell students to choose a game piece and roll the dice to decide in what order they will play (highest goes first).

To play the game, students should pick a Truth Telling card from the stack, read it aloud and then determine what they would do if they were in that situation. If they would tell the truth and can verbalize a truth they would tell that wouldn't hurt others, they roll the dice and move their piece that many spaces. If they wouldn't tell the truth, then they stay where they are and the next player takes a turn. The catch here is that students have to be willing to be honest about whether they would really be truthful in that situation. The first one to the finish line wins.

Play until students complete the game or for as much time as you can allow, then tell students to choose one of the cards to take with them as a challenge to tell the truth this week. Close in prayer, giving students a few moments of silent reflection to think about situations where they might be tempted to lie this week and to ask God to help them tell the truth instead.

Option 2: From Lies to Praise. For this option, you need Bibles, index cards, a worship CD or mp3 and a player, and pens or pencils.

Ask for a volunteer to read 1 Peter 5:8, then explain that, if you're a Christian, you have an enemy. He's mean and violent and he wants you to fail. He will try to get you into situations where the "easy" way out will be to lie. Because of him, you have to be extra careful.

Ask for another volunteer to read James 3:8-10 while students follow along. Emphasize that we can't tame our tongues, but God can. One way to let God tame our tongues is to fill it with praises of Him. Instead of using our tongues for lying, as we've talked about today, or gossip or swearing, we can use it to bless God.

Distribute index cards and pens or pencils, and tell students to write "I will praise God for . . ." at the top of their card. Ask them to begin listing reasons they will praise God, and remind them that even as they think of praises, God is praised.

As students work, play some worship music. (If you're musical, you could also lead a time of praise and worship when they're done.) Close by asking students to pray some of their praises of God aloud. Remind students to take their cards with them and to fill their mouths with honest praises rather than lies.

REFLECT

The following short devotions are for the students to reflect on and answer during the week. You can make a copy of these pages and distribute to your class or print out from the PDF available online at **www.gospellight.com/ uncommon_jh_parents_and_family.zip**.

1—THE TROUBLE WITH TRUTH

Ephesians 4:21-23 is all about old and new. Which are you?

Kimber went with her friend Tracy to camp last summer. While she was there, she became a Christian. She loves Jesus so much! But she never knew how hard it would be to follow Him.

Before she decided to follow Jesus, Kimber lied all the time. Lying was totally normal. After all, how else was she supposed to keep from getting into trouble? When she got a bad grade, she faked her mom's signature on the note sent home by the teacher. No big deal. When she dinged Dad's car with her bike, she told him that she was pretty sure she saw Billy from across the street riding recklessly around the neighborhood. No problem.

Now things are different. She knows that lying and deceit are part of the *old* Kimber—and that the *new* Kimber, who wants to be like Jesus, tells the truth. But now she gets in trouble all the time! Instead of deceiving her way out of mistakes and messes, Kimber faces the consequences . . . and they are not always pleasant.

Have you ever told the truth and then regretted it when you had to face the consequences? Did you think maybe you would have been better off lying? Why?

_____

_____

_____

_____

_____

_____

Sometimes telling the truth hurts a lot worse than lying—but it really is the best thing to do. Take a minute to read Romans 8:28. When you pray today, ask God to show you how He is using the trouble in your life for good.

2—DON'T MENTION IT

If you're hoping for a good day, 1 Peter 3:10 is the best place to start.

Hakim's parents gave him permission to stay the night at his friend Marty's house on Friday night. When he got there, Hakim discovered that Marty's parents, Mr. and Mrs. Sanderson, weren't home—they'd gone away for the weekend and left Marty's older brother, Darrel, in charge . . . and Darrel is having a party.

There are high school kids all over the house, and a lot of them are drinking. Hakim even walked in on a couple making out in the bathroom! Marty and Hakim are hanging out in Marty's room and playing video games—they're not joining the party or anything—but Hakim is pretty sure that if his parents knew what was going on, they would want him to come home immediately (and maybe even bring Marty with him). But it's not like he's lying if he just doesn't mention it, right?

What should Hakim do?

- ❏ Hang out with Marty in his room, and tomorrow tell his parents that's what he did
- ❏ Have Darrel call his parents to let them know Mr. and Mrs. Sanderson aren't home, but he will keep an eye on Marty and Hakim
- ❏ Call his parents and tell them exactly what's going on

None of the options are outright lies, but only one is actually honest. Neglecting to tell the *whole* truth is sometimes just as deceitful as telling a lie. Is there an area of your life where you're being less than honest? Why are you hiding the truth?

_____

_____

_____

_____

If you are afraid to tell the whole truth, write a short prayer below, asking God to give you strength and courage to do what you know is right.

_____

_____

_____

_____

3—THE RIGHT WAY

Check out 1 Peter 3:15 to find out the right way to tell the truth.

Sometimes it seems impossible to tell the truth without being mean! The apostle Peter knew it could be tricky, and he offered this advice (fill in the blanks):

Always be prepared to _____ _____ _____ to everyone who _____ you to give the _____ for the hope that you have. But do this with _____ and _____ (1 Peter 3:15).

It's important to be prepared for truth-telling . . . and it's just as important to prepare ourselves to be gentle and respectful. Ephesians 4:15 calls this combination "speaking the truth in love."

Can you think of a time when you told the truth and it came out all wrong? What could you have said instead, with gentleness and respect?

_____

_____

_____

_____

Did you know that *gentleness* is one of the fruits of the Spirit? Check out Galatians 5:22-23 and write down three of the fruits that will help you be more truthful. How will you grow those fruits in your life this week?

_____

_____

_____

_____

4—TRUTH AND WISDOM

Wanna win big? Then read what to avoid in Proverbs 17:20.

The book of Proverbs is an ancient book of Hebrew wisdom, sayings passed down from father to son, mother to daughter, to make sure the next generation has the tools they need for healthy and successful lives. Many proverbs address the importance of honesty and truth-telling—and a lot of them warn about the dangers of lying, too!

If you're ready to fill up on wisdom for life, try this: Read one chapter of Proverbs every day. There are 31 chapters, just enough to get you through one month. Each day, pick one verse from that day's chapter that really speaks to your life, and then memorize it. Before long, you'll have a stockpile of wisdom for just about every occasion.

Here's another idea: Ask your family to read and memorize Proverbs together. With God's Word growing inside each one of you, speaking the truth in love will get easier every day!

AFTER YOU

THE BIG IDEA

Family members and friends put each other first.

SESSION AIMS

In this session, you will guide students to (1) understand the benefits of sacrifice; (2) feel motivated to serve others; and (3) plan specific ways to put others first this week.

THE BIGGEST VERSE

"Now that I, your Lord and Teacher, have washed your feet, you also should wash one another's feet" (John 13:14).

OTHER IMPORTANT VERSES

Genesis 13; Psalm 62:5-8; Mark 14:35-36; Acts 20:35; Philippians 2:3-11

Note: Additional options and worksheets in 8¹/₂" x 11" format for this session are available for download at **www.gospellight.com/uncommon_jh_parents_and_family.zip**.

STARTER

Option 1: Family Time. For this option, you need junior high students who like to hang out with family members.

Greet students and ask them to think of—but not say—an activity they would like to do with their family on a Saturday afternoon. Explain that one common problem families run into is trying to decide how to spend time together. On your signal, students should find a partner and each say what they would like to do. Partners can try to convince each other to participate in their activity, but they should work at finding an agreement. If they can't agree how to spend time, they can move on to another partner. As pairs agree, ask them to sit together.

Ask for a show of hands of (1) how many got their partner to agree to the activity they originally had in mind, (2) how many compromised to an activity neither had thought of beforehand, and (3) how many gave up what they wanted to do in favor of their partner's activity.

Now discuss the following:

- How often do you face a situation like this with your family?
- How do you typically handle it?
- Have you ever known someone who always insisted on doing what they wanted? How did that make you feel?
- Do you think you usually put yourself or others first? How does that affect your relationships?

Explain that family members put each other first, which means they're willing to not get their way sometimes in order that other family members get what they want. But as we'll see today, in the end, their relationship grows because of it.

Option 2: Putting Each Other First. For this option, you need active participants and some space to move around.

Greet students and ask them to form even teams of six to eight and sit in a circle on the floor with their team. Tell teams that you will call out a series of descriptive statements, such as "someone who owns a dog." Teams should discuss amongst themselves who in their group fits the statement, and then line up single file behind that person. The first team done receives two points. If the statement describes no one on their team, they remain seated. After each round, teams should sit in a circle again.

However, the goal is to line up behind a different person each time. If some-one from their team has to be first more than once and they win that round, their team will receive one point instead of two.

There's one more catch: students can't volunteer to be first. In order to choose the person who goes first, someone who *does not* fit the statement should ask their teammates whether they do. Only then can someone say, "Yes, I own a dog." Or someone can volunteer a teammate, for example, "Janie, I know you own a dog." In other words, the *team* puts someone first rather than individuals putting themselves first.

Read the following list of statements:

- Someone who is an only child.
- Someone who likes art.
- Someone who hates math.
- Someone who has a good relationship with their parents at the moment.
- Someone who got all *As* on their last report card.
- Someone who has met someone famous.
- Someone who has lived in the same house their whole life.
- Someone who has visited a different country.
- Someone who plays a musical instrument.
- Someone who has a grandparent living with them.

You may need to prepare additional statements that will fit your group. Play until you have a clear winner. Ask others to line up behind the winning team and applaud wildly for them. Then discuss the following:

- How did it feel not to be able to volunteer yourself?
- What can family members or friends do to put each other first? How important are those things in a relationship?
- How might your relationships change if you volunteered yourself less to be first and your family and friends more?

Summarize by explaining that family members and friends can put each other first by focusing more on what others want than what they want. We'll see both *why* and *how* to do that today.

MESSAGE

Option 1: Giving Gifts. For this option, you need Bibles, a small gift for every student (plus a few extras) and a bag of wrapped candies.

Ahead of time, you'll need to prepare small gifts. They can be as simple or elaborate as you'd like. For example, you can create gift certificates for a soda—your treat—and put them inside envelopes. Or you can gather small gift boxes (typically available at craft stores) and fill them with candies. Gifts don't have to be the same, but should be generic so that whoever receives them can use them. This activity will work best if students can't tell what the gifts are by looking at them.

Ask students to sit in a circle. With sincerity, gush at students about how much you enjoy being their youth leader. Include specific group memories that bring you special joy. Tell junior-highers that you feel so privileged to spend time with them that you brought a present for each of them.

Pass out a gift to each person, but ask him or her not to open it. As students hold their gift, ask them to consider this question: *Would you like to give a gift to someone sitting in this circle?* If they answer yes, they can get up and give away the present they have. Keep track of any who give away their gifts. Some students may end up with several presents, while others may have none. On the other hand, your students may all choose to keep the gifts you gave them. After the gift "exchange" and before students open their presents, ask:

- How did you feel when I gave you your gift?
- What made you decide whether you would keep or give away your present?
- How do you think others feel about your choice?

Pass out Bibles and ask students to take turns around the circle reading a verse of Genesis 13 until they've read the entire chapter.

Explain that you put the students first by giving them gifts. But you also gave them a gift of freedom: a choice to put someone else first. Some of them accepted the first gift, while others accepted the second gift by following your lead and putting someone else first.

Hand another gift and a few wrapped candies to any students who gave away their gifts. Continue by explaining that Abram put Lot first by allowing Lot to choose first the land he wanted. God blessed Abram's decision by promising Abram all the land he could see, including the land Lot chose. That did happen—Abram became Abraham and his descendants, the Jews, are vast and numerous! Just like God blessed Abram for giving Lot the first choice of land, you are "blessing" with a similar gift and some candy those students who gave away their gift.[1]

Option 2: Cramped Spaces. For this option, you need Bibles and masking tape. Ahead of time, tape a three-foot by three-foot square on the floor for every 10 students you anticipate attending, plus one or two more to be safe.

Ask students to form groups of 10 and gather around a square. Explain that you will read a Bible story and ask students to step one by one into the square to represent characters. Group members will need to touch each other and accommodate their growing discomfort as their square fills up. Everyone should keep both feet inside the square while their character is in it, and then exit the square when their character exits the story.

Read Genesis 13 and then add characters as follows: Abram, Abram's wife, Lot (v. 1); Abram's livestock (v. 2); the Lord (v. 4); Lot's flocks and herds (v. 5); Abram's herdsmen, Lot's herdsmen, the Canaanites and the Perizzites (v. 7). Characters can exit as follows: Lot, Lot's flocks and herds, Lot's herdsmen (v. 11); Abram, Abram's wife, Abram's livestock, Abram's herdsmen (v. 12); the Lord (v. 14).

After the reading, ask students to sit as you discuss the following:

- What problem did Abram and Lot have? *There were too many people and animals in a small space (see v. 6).*
- How did they handle the problem? *Abram suggested they part ways, and he let Lot choose his land first (see vv. 8-9).*
- What did Abram sacrifice for Lot's sake? *He could have chosen whatever land he wanted, but he let Lot choose first.*
- Did Abram make a good decision? Why or why not? *Yes. He solved the problem by putting Lot first, and God blessed him as a seal of approval (see vv. 11-12, 14-17).*
- How did God respond to Abram's decision? *God promised to give Abram and his countless offspring all the land he could see in every direction, which would include the land Lot had just chosen (see vv. 14-17).*

Youth Leader Tip

If you have less than 12 students, tape one 3x3-foot square and have everyone participate. However, if you have more than 12 students, tape additional squares and do this activity in groups. (You'll want to tape smaller squares if you have less than 10 people.)

- Why do you think God blessed Abram? *Abram made two wise decisions: he put God first when he worshiped the LORD (see vv. 3-4), and then he put Lot first (see v. 8).*

Explain that Abram could have acted selfishly and chosen his land first. But he showed that he was more concerned about others by letting Lot, his nephew, choose the land he wanted. God honors sacrifice and blessed Abram for his wise decision. Abram became Abraham and his descendants, the Jews, are vast and numerous!

DIG

Option 1: *Rudy*. For this option, you will need a copy of the film *Rudy*, a TV, a DVD player and Bibles. (*Note*: this film is rated PG, so be sure to pay attention to any objectionable language or content as you show this carefully selected scene to your students.)

Ahead of time, cue the movie to the scene where football players turn in their jerseys one by one to the coach, asking that Rudy play in their place in the next game (approximately one hour and 33 minutes from the opening Columbia TriStar Pictures graphic). The scene lasts about a minute, ending with Rudy on the phone, explaining to his dad that he'll be on the bench in uniform.

Explain that the movie *Rudy* is based on the true story of Rudy Ruettiger, a guy who grew up dreaming of playing football for the University of Notre Dame. Despite his struggles with academics and finances, plus the fact that he had little athletic ability, his determination inspired others and paid off. Because the team was so big and league rules only allowed a certain number of players to wear uniforms during a game, Rudy didn't have a chance even to sit on the bench without playing, let alone play.

Show the clip, and then discuss the following:

- Would you have been willing to sit out the big game just so a teammate could sit on the bench? Why or why not?
- Have you ever given up something you really wanted for a family member or a friend? Describe that experience.
- Read 1 John 3:16-17, and then ask, "How did the football players demonstrate the principle of this passage?" (*At least for one football game, they were willing to lay down their right to play so that Rudy could wear the uniform.*)
- What else in your life might God ask you to lay down for others?[2]

Option 2: The Bear and the Travelers. For this option, you need three corny actor-types, a chair to represent a tree and a Bible.

Ask for three volunteers to pantomime as you read the following adaptation of Aesop's fable "The Bear and the Travelers." Two will portray students and one will portray the bear. (Choose someone who will really act it up to play the bear.) Place the chair at an appropriate spot to represent the tree.

Two junior-highers went for a walk in the woods. Suddenly, a bear appeared. Before the bear saw them, one junior-higher ran to a tree, climbed into the branches and hid. The other was not as quick and couldn't climb as well, so he threw himself on the ground and played dead. The bear came up and sniffed all around him, but the student held his breath and kept still. The bear thought he was dead and went away. After the bear had gone, the junior-higher in the tree came down and asked her companion what the bear had whispered to him. The other replied, "He told me not to hang out with a friend who deserts you at the first sign of danger."[3]

Ask your volunteers to take a bow, and then discuss:

- Who did you most relate to in this story? Explain.
- Would you have done anything differently? If so, what?
- Did anyone put anyone else first in this story?
- How could the junior-higher in the tree have put her friend first? What do you think held her back from doing so? What would she have risked by putting her friend first? Is that a risk worth taking?

Read Romans 12:10, and then ask:

- How might this story have been different if the students had known this verse?
- What can junior high students do to "honor one another above" themselves?
- What gets in the way of doing those things?

Explain that we could come up with lots of excuses—including personal safety—for putting ourselves first. But God doesn't promise safety as we follow Jesus. Jesus was willing to give up His life for others, and He might ask that of us, too. The question is whether we are willing to follow God by putting Him and others first at any cost.

APPLY

Option 1: Friendly Ideas. For this option, you need Bibles, index cards and pens or pencils.

Ask students to form small groups of three to five and open their Bibles to Proverbs 18:1a. Allow a volunteer to read it as everyone follows along. Explain that if "an unfriendly man pursues selfish ends," then it makes sense that a friendly person pursues the good of others.

Give each person a pen or pencil and each group a stack of index cards. Instruct groups to brainstorm things junior-highers could do this week to put others first (for example, doing an extra chore or not pushing ahead in the lunch line). Ask them to write one friendly thing on each card; that one friendly thing should be broad enough that most everyone could do it (for example, "Help out my 11 brothers and sisters" is probably applicable to only a few junior-highers, but "Help out a family member" is probably relevant to all).

When groups have at least one idea from each person in their group, collect the cards, shuffle them and hand them out again. Ask students to read their card, then discuss with their group how they will live that suggestion this week. For example, if the card suggests doing an extra chore, they might plan to clear the dinner table each night this week or mow the lawn on Saturday. Encourage students to write their specific plan on their card.

After a few minutes for discussion, close in prayer, asking that the Spirit would continue to challenge students this week with ideas for how they can put others first.

Option 2: What Will You Sacrifice? For this option, you need magazines, paper, scissors, tape or glue, Bibles and markers.

Youth Leader Tip
Presenting students with opportunities to serve others and challenging them with Bible lessons will go far in helping them process their responsibilities in relationships, in life, and in God's kingdom.

Ahead of time, cut out magazine pictures of things that are important—maybe even *too* important—to junior-highers, such as friends, TV, video games, computers, popular music artists, sports and physical appearance.

Hold up each picture and explain how you've noticed that the thing, person, activity or whatever pictured is important to junior-highers. (For example, some students are so committed to soccer that they miss church to go to games, or others are so into physical appearance that they spend more time getting ready than they do with their family.) Explain that while none of these things is bad in itself, it can become a problem if we make it too important. Ask, "How do these things get in the way of our relationships?" (*We spend more time on them, think about them more, choose to do them or have them instead of spending time with people.*)

After a few minutes, ask students to open their Bibles to John 15:12-13 and read it aloud together. Explain that because He loved us, Jesus sacrificed His very life in order to put us, His friends, first. He asks us to love our family and friends in the same way, by laying down our lives, too. Are you willing to lay down your life so that others can come to know Jesus? What are you willing to give up to allow others to know Him—appearances, reputation, comfort?

One at a time, hold up each picture in the air for 15-30 seconds, and let students silently pray that that thing will not be more important than laying down his or her life to reach out to others. If they feel it is more important, they should confess that to God and ask Him to change their attitude. When you're done with all the items, thank God for the way Jesus laid down His life for us and ask Him to give us that same kind of grace-filled commitment and courage.

REFLECT

The following short devotions are for the students to reflect on and answer during the week. You can make a copy of these pages and distribute to your class or print out from the PDF available online at **www.gospellight.com/ uncommon_jh_parents_and_family.zip**.

1—SHARE AND SHARE ALIKE

Jesus says something important in Luke 3:11. (If you're not sure what a tunic is, look it up!)

Mandy has a lot of clothes. A *lot*. Mandy's mom loves to shop, and is a genius at finding super-cute fashions at incredible bargains.

Danielle, one of Mandy's friends from youth group, does not have a lot of clothes. Her dad lost his job and hasn't been able to find another one, and Danielle hasn't had anything new for a year or more. She rotates her outfits between three shirts and two pairs of jeans.

Mandy thinks it would be really wonderful to share her clothes with Danielle. They're the same size, so sharing would be a cinch. She asked her mom if that would be okay and Mom said yes . . . but Mandy's not sure how to bring up the subject with Danielle. She wants to help her friend, not make her feel embarrassed!

What can Mandy say or do to let Danielle know she wants to share?

_____

_____

_____

_____

Do you know someone who needs something you have? Is there a way you can share that will make both of you feel good?

_____

_____

_____

_____

Our culture tends to look down on people who don't have much, which sometimes makes it hard to share . . . but Jesus was pretty clear that when we have things that others need, we have to find a way. Talk with your parents, a youth leader or your pastor this week about ways you can help!

2—RATED G FOR "GIVING"

Don't be selfish! Check out Philippians 2:3.

Every other Saturday afternoon, Casey's family—him, his mom and his brother, Connor—go to a movie and then share a banana split at Scoop-A-Rama. It's their thing, and all three of them look forward to hanging out and doing something fun together.

Mom has final approval, but either Casey or Connor gets to pick which movie to see, depending on who won the Chores Challenge during the past two weeks. Casey won this time by a mile (he had done the dishes *every single night!*) and is totally amped to see the film of his choice, which is an extremely cool kung-fu movie that all his friends have already seen.

But Connor is feeling low after a rough week at school, and Casey wonders if he can do something to cheer his brother up. He knows that Connor has really been looking forward to a new documentary about polar bears, which is also playing at the theater. Casey isn't really into nature movies or polar bears, but he feels a nudge in his heart telling him to put Connor first.

At the box office counter, Mom turns to Casey. "So what's it gonna be, King of the Chores Challenge?"

If you were Casey, what would you say next?

- ❏ "Kung-fu today. Kung-fu forever!"
- ❏ "I feel like visiting the North Pole. Don't they have polar bears?"
- ❏ "Let's skip the banana split and see a double feature. Wouldn't it be awesome if polar bears knew kung-fu?"

Think of a family member or friend who needs encouragement. What can you do this week to put that person before yourself?

_____

_____

_____

_____

_____

3—THE LORD'S SHARE

Read Malachi 3:10. It's time to give the Lord His share!

Try something different today. Look up the word "share" in a Bible dictionary or online at Biblegateway.com. When you do, you'll find something interesting. Nearly every time the word appears in Scripture, it's used as a noun, not a verb. Like in Leviticus 6:22: "It is the LORD's regular share and is to be burned completely."

In ancient times, the Israelites offered burnt offerings to God. They called this offering a "tithe," and a tithe was 10-percent of everything they had. If they had 10 sheep, one of them was given to God as His share. If they had 10 pounds of olives from their groves, one pound was given to God. The Israelites made this sacrifice for two reasons: (1) because God commanded it, and (2) because it reminded them that everything they had was a gift from the Lord.

The Church has adopted this very healthy habit. No, we don't burn offerings anymore, because Jesus' death on the cross is the only sacrifice we need for the forgiveness of our sins. But we do tithe, for the same reasons the Israelites did: God says to do it, and we need a regular reminder that everything we have is from Him. In addition, giving a portion of our money, time and talents is a really good way to put God and others before ourselves. When we give to God and His people before pleasing ourselves, we've got our priorities straight.

Below is the formula for figuring out your tithe of money. (You can use the same formula to figure out your tithe of time and talents by substituting hours-per-week for dollars-per-week. Add up your hours of free-time per week for "time" and your hours of sports, music, drama or other practice per week for "talents.")

dollars per week _____ X .10 = _____ my tithe (10 percent)

Write the amount of your tithe on the lines below, and then talk to your parents, a youth leader or your pastor about how to give your tithe to God.

Money tithe = _____

Time tithe =   _____

Talents tithe = _____

4—THE TWO MAIN THINGS

I command you to check out Matthew 22:37-38. (Pretty please?)

Fill in the blanks below:

"_____ the Lord your God with all your _____ and with all your _____ and with all your _____." This is the _____ and _____ commandment. And the second is like it: "_____ your neighbor as yourself" (Matthew 22:37-38).

There are a lot of commands in the Bible. The Ten Commandments (found in Exodus 20) are the biggies, of course, but there are a lot of others too. On top of that, there's a ton of good advice that isn't exactly commanded, but *is* strongly recommended for anyone who wants to live a godly life (the book of Proverbs is a good example).

Do you ever feel like you can't keep it all straight? If so, take a deep breath—there's no need to feel overwhelmed. In the verses above, Jesus gives us the key to pleasing God: loving Him and loving others. All of the Bible's other commands and advice are guidelines for how best to obey these two commandments.

What is one way you will love God this week?

_____
_____
_____
_____
_____
_____

What is one way you will love others this week?

_____
_____
_____
_____
_____
_____

Memorize these two verses this week. Better yet, invite your family to memorize them with you. As you take these commandments into your heart and practice obeying them, you'll experience the peace that comes with knowing that you're living God's way.

CAN WE TALK?

THE BIG IDEA

Family members and friends confront each other about wrongdoing.

SESSION AIMS

In this session, you will guide students to (1) learn that appropriate confrontation can be positive and helpful; (2) feel increasingly comfortable about the act of confronting another; and (3) pray for the willingness to confront in love when necessary.

THE BIGGEST VERSE

"Let the word of Christ dwell in you richly as you teach and admonish one another with all wisdom, and as you sing psalms, hymns and spiritual songs with gratitude in your hearts to God" (Colossians 3:16).

OTHER IMPORTANT VERSES

2 Samuel 12:1-10; Proverbs 17:17; John 16:7-11; Romans 15:14; Hebrews 1:1-2

Note: Additional options and worksheets in 8$^1/_2$" x 11" format for this session are available for download at **www.gospellight.com/uncommon_jh_parents_and_family.zip**.

STARTER

Option 1: Falling Down. For this option, you need enough humility to share about a really embarrassing fall.

Share about a time when you took an embarrassing but spectacular fall—the more dramatic the better. (For example, maybe your mountain bike got going too fast and you took a wrong turn down the steepest part of the hill, narrowly missed a tree but landed smack in poison ivy.) If at the end there was someone to help you up, that would be a bonus.

Invite others to share their falling-down stories. Be sure to laugh *with* and not *at* volunteers. Then discuss:

- Other than physically, how do junior-highers fall down, meaning they make mistakes? *They make poor choices to do things like cheat, lie to their parents or drink.*
- What do you do when your family members or friends fall, meaning make mistakes?
- Does it make a difference in the way you handle it whether they realize they're blowing it or not?
- How has a family member or friend helped you when you've fallen?
- What do you think it means to confront someone?
- How can junior high students confront a family member or friend in a positive way? (Don't expect students to have all the right answers at this point—if they did, you wouldn't need to teach this lesson!)

Explain that everyone falls down. It's embarrassing and often it hurts. But it also gives others an opportunity to help us up again. As we'll see today, when your family members or friends fall, you might have the opportunity to help them by confronting them and helping them deal with their problems.

Option 2: Out of Control. For this option, you need four paper bags, four copies of "Out of Control" (found on the next page) and a large playing space. Ahead of time, cut each handout into slips of paper and put one full set in each of the paper bags. Clear your room as much as possible or go outside to play this game.

Greet students and ask them to form four teams and gather in four corners of the playing area. Tell students that they'll compete in a relay race to get their whole team from their corner into the opposite diagonal corner. Give each team a paper bag with instructions. Explain that the first person on each team

OUT OF CONTROL

Run ahead fast.	Leapfrog to the opposite corner.
Run backward.	Shuffle (don't let your feet leave the floor).
Crawl.	Skip.
Squat and waddle like a duck.	Spin in circles.
Lay down and roll.	Hold your ankles as you walk.

will draw a piece of paper from their bag and race to the opposite corner in the manner described on the paper. (He or she should return the card to the bag once he or she has read it, to ensure that everyone on the team gets a chance.) Once the first person reaches the opposite corner, the second person can reach inside the bag and grab instructions, and so on. When each player reaches the opposite corner, he or she should sit down. Play continues until three of the four teams have finished.

This game gets confusing because all four teams have to cross the center of the room while doing different things. Ask students to be aware of each other and how they interact with each other as they pass.

After the game, discuss:

- How did you interact as you bumped into each other (for example, did you apologize or tell others to watch out)?
- How do you typically deal with it when someone bumps into you, say at school or at the mall?
- Other than physically, how do family members or friends bump into each other (meaning they make mistakes that often affect others)?
- What effect did your speed have on whether or not you bumped into others?
- How is that like life?

Explain that sometimes people allow circumstances or bad decisions to get them going too quickly and headed for danger. As we'll see today, one positive way to handle someone who's out of control is to confront him or her with his or her behavior. The person may not even realize that he or she has a problem until you respectfully tell him or her.[1]

MESSAGE

Option 1: Second Samuel Skit. For this option, you need copies of the "Nathan's Story" script (found on the following two pages), a royal-looking robe (you define the term—it could be a bed sheet or old bathrobe), lots of cotton balls and a paper crown.

Choose volunteers to play the following roles: Narrator, Nathan and David are speaking roles; Rich man, Poor man, Saul, several girls as wives, Uriah and Bathsheba are non-speaking roles. Explain that the actors with speaking parts will use non-speaking actors as props, and non-speakers should react to the

Characters

Narrator
Nathan
David
Rich man
Poor man
Saul
Several girls
Uriah
Bathsheba

Props
Royal-looking robe
cotton balls
paper crown

Narrator: The LORD sent Nathan to David. When he came to him, he said . . .

Nathan: There were two men in a certain town [ARRANGE THE TWO VOLUNTEERS AS PROPS], one rich [PUT A ROBE ON HIM] . . .

Rich man: [LOOK HAPPY WITH YOUR WEALTH.]

Nathan: . . . and the other poor [SHRUG YOUR SHOULDERS AND SHOW HIM EMPTY HANDS].

Poor man: [LOOK SAD AT YOUR EMPTY HANDS.]

Nathan: The rich man had a very large number of sheep and cattle [GIVE HIM LOTS AND LOTS OF COTTON BALLS] . . .

Rich man: [REJOICE IN YOUR COTTON BALLS.]

Nathan: . . . but the poor man had nothing [SHRUG AT HIM AGAIN] except one little ewe lamb he had bought [LOOK HAPPY AS YOU GIVE HIM ONE COTTON BALL].

Poor man: [LOOK LOVINGLY AT YOUR COTTON BALL. AS NATHAN READS, DO WHAT HE SAYS AS MUCH AS POSSIBLE.]

Nathan: He raised it, and it grew up with him and his children. It shared his food, drank from his cup and even slept in his arms. It was like a daughter to him. Now a traveler came to the rich man [PUT THE TRAVELER NEXT TO THE RICH MAN], but the rich man refrained from taking one of his own sheep or cattle to prepare a meal for the traveler who had come to him.

Rich man: [GUARD YOUR OWN COTTON BALLS, AND THEN SNEAK OVER TO THE POOR MAN AND TAKE HIS LAMB.]

Nathan: Instead, he took the ewe lamb that belonged to the poor man and prepared it for the one who had come to him.

Poor man: [LOOK HORRIFIED AT THE RICH MAN, THEN HEARTBROKEN AT YOUR EMPTY HANDS.]

Narrator: David burned with anger against the man and said to Nathan . . .

David: [BURN WITH ANGER!] As surely as the LORD lives, the man who did this [POINT AT THE RICH MAN] deserves to die! He must pay for that lamb four times over, because he did such a thing and had no pity.

Narrator: Then Nathan said to David . . .

Nathan: [POINT AT DAVID] You are the man!

David: [LOOK SHOCKED.]

Nathan: This is what the LORD, the God of Israel, says: "I anointed you king over Israel [PUT A CROWN ON DAVID'S HEAD] . . .

Saul: [GRAB DAVID IN A HEADLOCK.]

Nathan: . . . and I delivered you from the hand of Saul [RELEASE DAVID FROM SAUL'S GRASP]. I gave your master's house to you . . .

Saul: [STAND WITH SOME GIRLS.]

Nathan: . . . and your master's wives into your arms [LEAD THE GIRLS TO DAVID]. I gave you the house of Israel and Judah. And if all this had been too little, I would have given you even more. Why did you despise the word of the LORD by doing what is evil in his eyes?

Uriah and Bathsheba: [STAND TOGETHER.]

Nathan: You struck down Uriah the Hittite with the sword . . .

David: [PRETEND TO STRIKE URIAH, AND THEN TAKE BATHSHEBA TO STAND NEXT TO YOU AND THE OTHER GIRLS.]

Nathan: . . . and took his wife to be your own. You killed him with the sword of the Ammonites. Now, therefore, the sword will never depart from your house, because you despised me and took the wife of Uriah the Hittite to be your own.

[ALL ACTORS FREEZE.]

story according to the script. (If you don't have enough students to fill the roles, you can read the role of Narrator and simply skip Saul's wives altogether.)

Encourage remaining students to participate as they would in a melo-drama, by exclaiming "Ooh!" "Aah!" "Boo! Hiss!" and "Hooray!" when it seems appropriate. While actors review their roles, lead the group in a few practice responses before beginning the drama. (You might choose a particularly confident student to act as a cheerleader of sorts for the rest of the group.) Then ask your thespians to present the skit. After the drama, discuss:

- What did David do wrong that needed confronting? *Rather than appreciate what God had already given him, he took what was not his to take. He had Uriah killed and took Uriah's wife as his own. He ignored God and His word and did what God considers evil (vv. 7-9).* (Make sure students understand the connection between Nathan's parable and David's sins.)
- Why did Nathan confront David? *Because the LORD sent him (see v. 1).*
- What did you notice about the way in which Nathan confronted David? *He used a story to help David understand why he had acted wrongly; he didn't speak from anger, but rather he said what God said and not what he thought.*
- Do you think Nathan acted as a friend to David? Why or why not?
- Would Nathan have acted as David's friend if he knew about David's sins and ignored them? Explain.
- If you were David, how would you respond to Nathan's confrontation? Explain.

Option 2: *The Lion King.* For this option, you need Bibles, a TV, a DVD player and a copy of the movie *The Lion King*.

Ahead of time, cue the video to the scene where Simba and Nala reunite in the jungle, about one hour after the opening Walt Disney Pictures graphic. The scene lasts one minute and 40 seconds and ends with Simba stalking off.

Ask students to open their Bibles to 2 Samuel 12:1-10 and choose five volunteers to read two verses each. When they're done, show the clip. Afterward, discuss the following:

- How are Nala and Nathan alike? *They both confront a friend who has blown it; both speak on behalf of others.* How are they different? *Nathan speaks for God, whereas Nala speaks for the pride of lions; Nathan tells*

David what will happen as a consequence for his sins, but Nala explains what has already happened because of Simba's desertion of the pride lands; Nathan might be gentler than Nala and is definitely more formal.

- How are Simba and David alike? *They are both royalty who have forgotten to act royal; both have been hiding their sins.* How are they different? *Simba thinks he killed Mufasah, but David really did kill Uriah to get Bathsheba for his own; David's sin is done, but Simba continues to sin (by shirking his responsibilities as king); Simba got angry and sulked off, but David confesses.* (Encourage students to come back next week to learn about David's response!)

- Who do you relate to most: Nala, Nathan, Simba or David? Explain. Do you think Nala and Nathan confront Simba and David out of friendship? Why or why not? What did Nala and Nathan risk to confront Simba and David? Do you think it was worth the risks?

- Do you think Nathan acted as a friend to David? Why or why not? Would Nathan have acted as David's friend if he knew about David's sins and ignored them? Explain. If you were David, how would you respond to Nathan's confrontation? Explain.

DIG

Option 1: Tasty Mud. For this option, you need a child-sized beach bucket and shovel, plastic spoons, chocolate pudding, chocolate sandwich cookies (such as Oreos) and Bibles.

Ahead of time, make the pudding. When it has set, crush the cookies (not too fine—you want some chunks) and mix them with the pudding so that you have a mixture that looks like mud. Put the mix in the beach bucket, but don't let students see it until this part of the lesson.

Bring out the bucket and tell students you mixed up a little mud. Using the shovel, pick some up and let it drop back in the bucket so students can see it. Ask for a volunteer to taste it, and then report their reaction. Pass out spoons to those who'd like a bite. Explain that the mud tastes better than students thought it would, and the same is true when it comes to confronting our family and friends. It's usually not as bad as we fear it's going to be. Then discuss:

- How do you feel about God asking you to confront others? Explain.
- What seems difficult about confrontation?

- Our culture says, "Mind your own business." What would be the results if everyone minded their own business?
- Why do you think God wants you to get involved in someone else's problem?

Ask if anyone would like to give a testimony about the benefits of confrontation. (It's probably best to ask them not to name names or get too specific.) Ask for volunteers to read Proverbs 13:17 and 17:17, and then discuss:

- What do these verses have to do with confrontation? *A trustworthy family member or friend can help you find healing from a bad situation.*

- Why does the character of the person confronting matter? *Confrontation should speak God's truth into a situation. A person who doesn't know God will have trouble knowing God's truth.*

- Why is love important in confrontation? *Confrontation is not about judging someone, but telling him or her what God thinks. It should come from love and concern for that person. People need love all the time, but especially during the hard times.*

Explain that when we obey God by confronting someone about their sin out of love and concern for them, we have the opportunity to help them find healing. While the idea of confrontation may seem like mud, the results may be sweeter than we think.

Option 2: Practicing Confrontation. For this option, you need Bibles.

Ask students to sit with a partner and choose who will go first. Explain that you're going to read a situation, and you want them to role-play how they would confront their family member or friend. "You" in each situation is the person with the choice to confront their family member or friend, while their partner plays the one being confronted. Encourage students to actually role-play the situations as opposed to just discussing what they would do. Allow a minute or two for each situation.

- Situation 1: You are at your friend's house. On his floor, you see his history paper with a teacher's great big A on the front. He sees you notice it and confides that he actually copied a paper he found on the Internet. You . . .

- Situation 2: Your sister is having a slumber party next weekend. She has invited you and a few others from church, but has intentionally not invited Juanita because she doesn't like her that much. But your sister keeps talking about it at church, even in front of Juanita. You . . .

Ask for a few volunteers to share how they handled each situation, then ask:

- How did it feel to confront someone?
- What do you think you did well?
- What would you change about your confrontation if you had it to do over again?
- What did you learn from the way your partner confronted you?
- How do you feel about God using you to confront others? Explain.

Ask for volunteers to read Proverbs 13:17 and 17:17, and then discuss:

- What do these verses have to do with confrontation? *A trustworthy family member or friend can help you find healing from a bad situation.*
- Why does the character of the person confronting matter? *Confrontation should speak God's truth into a situation. A person who doesn't know God will have trouble knowing God's truth.*
- Why is love important in confrontation? *Confrontation is not about judging someone, but telling him or her what God thinks. It should come from love and concern for that person. People need love all the time, but especially during the hard times.*

Explain that confrontation can be a big deal, like it was when Nathan confronted David. But more often, God will ask you to confront family members or friends in everyday situations. You'll be best prepared on those occasions if you regularly take time to study and learn God's Word. Only then will you know what God thinks and how to share that with others.

APPLY

Option 1: Preparing in Prayer. For this option, you need Bibles.

Ask students to open their Bibles to Romans 15:14 and follow along as you read. Then explain that, just as Paul felt convinced that the Romans were full of goodness, complete in knowledge and competent to instruct one another, *you* are confident of those things for the students. As evidence, share group memories from times when you saw spiritual maturity in students' lives.

Then continue that the real reason you are confident is that you see evidence that students want to follow Jesus and that they will allow His Spirit to work in and through them. With God on their side, they won't go wrong.

Tell students to use this verse as a guide for prayer. Ask them first to spend some time alone confessing sin and asking for the Spirit to fill them up with goodness. After a minute, ask students to find partners and pray together for time and diligence to study God's Word and grow in knowledge from the church and other believers. After a minute, ask students to form groups of three and pray that the person on their left would be willing to confront others when God asks them to. Close the meeting in prayer, asking the Spirit's leading as the students continue to follow Jesus.

Option 2: The Ultimate Confrontation. For this option, you need Bibles, paper, index cards, pens or pencils and Bible study tools, such as concordances or Bible dictionaries. (*Note:* This option is designed as an extended follow-up to Option 1: "Preparing in Prayer.")

After the prayer time described in "Preparing in Prayer," explain that confronting someone with his or her sin only goes so far. If they don't know Jesus, they don't have an eternal hope or reason to change. Give each student a pen or pencil, a piece of paper and an index card. Ask students first to pray for specific family members or friends God has put on their heart during this lesson whom they need to confront.

Next, ask someone to read Colossians 3:16. Explain that before you teach and admonish (or confront) someone, you need to let God's Word dwell in you richly. Ask students to think of questions they need to answer for themselves before they feel prepared to confront people. (For example, maybe they would like to know exactly what the Bible says about drinking alcohol before they confront someone on that issue.) Ask them to list some questions on the paper, and then look to the Bible study tools for answers. (You may need to explain how these tools are best used.)

Encourage students to look for ways to connect the specific issues they research with the good news of the gospel. At this point, students may work in groups if they have similar questions or issues.

Finally, ask students to write unanswered questions on their index card and give it to you. Here's the hard part: You have to help them find the answers! You can do this in one of two ways. Either ask the students to write down their name on the card (and you can return the card to them with a written answer) or plan a question-and-answer time after the session to address students' questions.

REFLECT

The following short devotions are for the students to reflect on and answer during the week. You can make a copy of these pages and distribute to your class or print out from the PDF available online at **www.gospellight.com/ uncommon_jh_parents_and_family.zip**.

1—FIRST THINGS FIRST

Read Nehemiah 1:4. Sometimes problems are so tough that tears are an okay reaction.

Nehemiah was a Hebrew prophet who got some terrible news about Israel's capital city. The walls around Jerusalem, built to protect God's people from attack, had been torn down. The tragedy had happened as a result of the Israelites' disobedience to God. The people who still lived there were so depressed that they hadn't bothered to start rebuilding.

Nehemiah knew that he had to confront the Israelites about two things. First, they needed to repent of the sins that had led them to the brink of destruction. Second, they needed to make it right by rebuilding the walls of the city. So what did Nehemiah do first?

He prayed. Almost the whole first chapter of the book of Nehemiah records his prayer to God for the Israelite people. He also prayed that the Lord would pave the way toward complete restoration. (It's a pretty good prayer—you should check it out!)

Do you need to confront a family member or friend who has made a bad choice? First things first: Write a prayer on the lines below, asking God to give you the right words at the right time.

_____

_____

_____

_____

_____

_____

God can and will use you to heal and restore the people closest to you. But make sure you talk to Him before you talk to your family member or friend.

2—FAMILY DYNAMICS

Read up on the recipe for good family dynamics in Ephesians 5:21.

Living in a family can be tough, right? It's even tougher when one member of the family goes his or her own way and doesn't consider anyone else. Families work best when everybody's headed in the same direction, encouraging each other along the way.

When a member of the family does something you don't like, it can be hard to tell whether or not they're being selfish—especially if that person is your parent! Sometimes it may feel like Mom or Dad doesn't have your best interests in mind, like they're just making up rules to annoy you. But here's the thing: They probably know best.

Sure, they make mistakes. But most of the time, they carefully and lovingly consider each member of the family and base their decisions on what they believe to be best for everyone.

It's okay to disagree (respectfully!) with your parents, but it's not okay to disobey just because you disagree. Unless they ask you to do something that God's Word forbids, the Bible is clear about the importance of following their lead. When you don't, *you* are the family member who's going your own way and needs to be confronted. Not a happy thought, is it?

Are you submitting to your parents' authority as Scripture says? Spend some time in prayer today, asking the Holy Spirit to confront you with the truth and help you honor, respect and obey your parents.

3—LEAD BY EXAMPLE

Lead the way to 1 Corinthians 11.

Jake is bummed about the other guys on the baseball team. They act like total jerks. They bad-mouth the umpire, cuss at the coach and insult opposing teams. A couple of them have also started chewing tobacco, a habit Jake thinks is disgusting.

He is the only Christian on the team and really wants to show Jesus to the other guys. He is also the team captain and always gets to say a few words before each game. Jake knows that if the other guys were believers, he could just come right out and tell them their behavior is lame and they need to shape up. But he isn't sure if that is the right call, since they aren't Christians.

What's your advice to Jake?

- ❏ Use his pre-game speech to preach a sermon about hell
- ❏ Threaten to quit the team unless the other guys get it together
- ❏ Concentrate on his own behavior and set an example for the other guys
- ❏ Pray that the Holy Spirit will convict the other guys and give him an opportunity to share about Jesus

Sometimes the best way to confront others is with the power of your good example. Are you following Christ in a way that's obvious to everyone?

4—ACCOUNTABILITY

Consider this: Hebrews 10:24. Any ideas?

A great way for Christian friends to help each other live God's way is to form what is sometimes called an "accountability group." This is a group of believers who trust each other with their struggles, pray for each other and offer advice when it is needed. The idea is that, if Jesus' followers seek Him together, it's a lot less likely that one or more of them will get off track.

The first key to a great accountability group is *trust*. This means that whatever is said within the group is never a topic of gossip and is shared only with a parent, youth leader or pastor when adult guidance is needed. (If the group isn't sure how to help one of the members with a problem or struggle in a godly way, that's a good time to seek advice from a trusted adult.)

The second key to a great accountability group is *honesty*. When believers are honest with each other about their growth, discouragement or temptation, confrontations happen less frequently. Why? Because it's hard to get off track in your walk with God when you've got a few trusted friends to keep you going straight.

Do two things today: Talk with your youth leader or pastor about starting an accountability group, and pray that God will bring the right people together to keep you all going strong!

I
CONFESS

THE BIG IDEA
Family members and friends confess to one another and support each other.

SESSION AIMS
In this session, you will guide students to (1) understand the reasons for confession; (2) feel connected to other Christians in significant relationships; and (3) confess their sins and confess Christ as Savior.

THE BIGGEST VERSE
"Therefore confess your sins to each other and pray for each other so that you may be healed. The prayer of a righteous man is powerful and effective" (James 5:16).

OTHER IMPORTANT VERSES
2 Samuel 13-25; Proverbs 18:12; John 9:1-5; James 4:6-10; 1 John 1:5-10

Note: Additional options and worksheets in 8$^1/_2$" x 11" format for this session are available for download at **www.gospellight.com/uncommon_jh_parents_and_family.zip**.

STARTER

Option 1: Catch Me. For this option, you need copies of "Catch Me" (found on the next page) and a softball or throwing-sized beanbag. Ahead of time, copy and cut up the "Catch Me" handout so that each student will have one question.

Greet students and ask them to spread out around the room as you pass out questions. Explain that you'll start the game by tossing the ball to someone. That person should answer his or her question and then toss the ball to someone else. Play continues until everyone in the group has answered his or her question.

Instruct students to exchange questions after Round 1 so that they have a new question to answer. You can decide whether to play for a certain number of rounds or for a set amount of time. When the game is over, discuss:

- What interesting fact did you learn about someone?
- Were some of these questions harder to answer than others? If so, which ones and why?
- What question (not necessarily from the handout) would you not want a family member or friend to ask you? Is there anyone with whom you can talk about those things?

Explain that we all have things that we'd prefer others not know about us. Sometimes those things come from areas where we've blown it. As we'll see today, while we can always talk to God about those things, confessing them to a family member or friend can help us deal with the problems and move on.[1]

Option 2: In the Confessional. For this option, you need index cards and pens or pencils.

Greet students and ask them to form pairs as you distribute index cards and pens or pencils. Instruct pairs to spread out and quietly take turns interviewing each other for interesting and little-known facts. (For example, "What's the wildest thing you've ever done?" "What bad habits do you have?" "What's the best thing you've done for someone else?") During the interviews, the interviewer takes legible notes of what the interviewee says. Stress that students should not write any name on the card.

When each person has three to five facts about their partner, ask students to form groups of no more than six. Group members should put the cards in the center of the circle and then randomly pick one. If they get themselves or

CATCH ME

What has been one of your greatest accomplishments so far in life?	What do you dream of doing?
Who do you admire?	What bad habits do you have?
How would your family describe you?	Imagine your life 25 years from now. What does it look like?
If you could do something differently in your life, what would you do?	Describe your happiest day.
What possession do you treasure and why?	What makes you angry?

their partner, they should put it back in the middle of the circle and choose another. Ask students to take turns in their group reading the facts on their card, then guessing which group member they've described.

When groups have finished, discuss:

- What interesting fact did you learn about someone?
- What question are you glad your interviewer didn't ask? Is there a family member or friend with whom you can talk about those things?
- What does it mean to you to confess something?
- Have you ever had to confess to someone? Describe the experience.
- What keeps people from confessing more often?
- What might be some benefits to confession?

Explain that while confession may be difficult and uncommon, as we'll see today, family members and friends confess to each other in order to gain help with their problems and to experience God's love.[2]

MESSAGE

Option 1: Us in the Dark. For this option, you need Bibles.

Pass out Bibles and ask students to open to 1 John 1:5-10. Explain that you will read the passage aloud, but they should read aloud with you each time they see the words "we," "us," "ourselves" and "our." (For example, students would read the italicized words in verse 9: "If *we* confess *our* sins, he is faithful and just and will forgive *us our* sins and purify *us* from all unrighteousness.")

When the reading is done, explain that even though Jesus came to offer each one of us a relationship with God, He also intends for us to be involved in significant relationships with family members, friends and other Christians. Unfortunately, the reality of sin in our lives affects others whether we think it does or not.

Ask students to stand and clear the center of the room (or move to another clear area—you want room to move, but not unlimited room). Tell students that you will read the passage again while they walk around with each other. However, some of the time they'll have their eyes closed to represent their sinfulness. During those times, they should try to move around people without touching them. Other times, their eyes will be open to represent their fellowship with God and each other, and they can give each other high fives as they pass.

Read 1 John 1:5-10 as follows, emphasizing the instructions in brackets:

[STAND STILL WITH EYES CLOSED] This is the message we have heard from him and declare to you: God is light; in him there is no darkness at all. [WALK WITH EYES CLOSED] If we claim to have fellowship with him yet walk in the darkness, we lie and do not live by the truth. [WALK WITH EYES OPEN AND HIGH-FIVE OTHERS] But if we walk in the light, as he is in the light, we have fellowship with one another, and the blood of Jesus, his Son, purifies us from all sin. [WALK WITH EYES CLOSED] If we claim to be without sin, we deceive ourselves and the truth is not in us. [WALK WITH EYES OPEN AND HIGH-FIVE OTHERS] If we confess our sins, he is faithful and just and will forgive us our sins and purify us from all unrighteousness. [STAND WITH EYES CLOSED] If we claim we have not sinned, we make him out to be a liar and his word has no place in our lives.

Ask students to be seated, and then discuss:

- What happened as you mingled with your eyes shut?
- How is that like what happens when you sin?
- What difference does confession make?
- How often do you hear people admit to being a sinner? Why do you think people pretend that they don't sin?
- If people were more willing to talk about the fact of their sin and admit to specific sins, how might that change their relationships with family members, friends and others?

Explain that confession forces us to stop pretending that we don't sin. In fact, in confession we admit that we do sin and that we need Jesus to forgive our sins. While we can confess our sins straight to God, we also need to be honest with ourselves and with each other about our sin. The church isn't a place where perfect people gather; instead, it should be a safe place to talk about the struggles of our lives, to find support from others who also struggle and to come to Jesus together seeking forgiveness and purification from all our unrighteousness.

Option 2: I Will Catch You. For this option, you need Bibles.
Ask students to form small groups of four to six to read 2 Samuel 12:13-25. When they've read the passage, ask them to discuss these questions:

- Did David have to confess to Nathan? Why did he?
- How did Nathan support David?

Ask volunteers to share what their group discussed. Next, ask students to stand in pairs (preferably with someone about their own size. Be sensitive to students who might be quite a bit larger than others and partner them with an adult). Instruct them to stand just far enough apart that they can hold their arms straight ahead and touch fingertips. Ask one person to turn around and stand with their arms crossed over their chest. On a count of three, that person should fall backward into the waiting arms of their partner. Each person should take a turn falling and catching.

Read James 5:16, and then discuss:

- How did you feel about falling? Why?
- Was it difficult to catch your partner? Explain.
- How is confession like falling into someone's arms?
- How important is it to catch someone when they confess?
- Why do you think James advises the person who receives confession to pray?
- How did Nathan help David heal?
- How would David and Nathan's relationship have changed if David refused to confess? Explain.[3]

Explain that David could have blown Nathan off or even gotten rid of him like he did Uriah. He didn't have to confess to him, but David would have been foolish to mess with God.

David still had to pay the consequences of his sin when his son died. But God blessed David's confession and repentance with another son and with a friend who continued to support David. Nathan pronounced God's love for the child with the name "Jedidiah," which means "loved by the LORD."

DIG

Option 1: Tabloid Confessions. For this option, you need several celebrity gossip magazines and Bibles.

Show students the magazines, highlighting some of their favorite stars or some sensational confessions. Discuss:

- What's the purpose of these confessions? Who benefits from them?
- Why is society so interested in celebrity confessions? How sincere do you think they are?

- Do these confessions present themselves as interesting facts or as confession of sin? What's the difference?
- Do you think the stars gained any personal support for their struggles as a result? Why or why not?

Ask students to open their Bibles to James 4:6-10 and invite a volunteer to read it. Then ask the following:

- What do pride and humility have to do with sin and confession? *Pride gets us into sin and keeps us from admitting it. Confession requires the humility to admit that we've blown it and to trust someone else to help us.*
- What else keeps us from confessing our sins? *We are afraid that we will be judged; we are afraid that we will lose the trust or respect of a family member or friend.*
- Why does James say we should be sad? *Because of our sin—we should express true humility and repentance.*
- How is confession like washing your hands? *Confession washes sin from your life like soap washes dirt from your hands.*
- How can confessing to a family member, a friend or another believer help you submit to God and resist the devil? *It's humbling to admit your sin to someone. They can help you understand the seriousness of sin and the importance of following God.*
- Do you feel like there are sins God won't forgive? How can confession help to reassure you of God's forgiveness? *As another believer offers you forgiveness and love, you can be assured that God also offers you forgiveness and love.*

Explain that while these magazines may contain confessions, they aren't true confessions of sin. Your confessions will (hopefully!) be much less sensational, but also more sincere and bring about lasting change in the way you live.

Youth Leader Tip

Confession may involve an apology if someone has wronged another, but not always. For example, one person might confess to another that he or she struggles with a particular sin so that the other person can hold him or her accountable.

Option 2: A Painful Confession. For this option, you need just this here book. Read the following story:

Joey was an eighth grader who had a hard time in math. No matter how hard he studied, he couldn't remember what to do with decimals. On one particular test, he was struggling with question number 4. He happened, accidentally, to glance at the test of the person next to him. Maria had written down the number 46.5 as the answer, so he did the same. Later that day, Joey started feeling bad. So he went and told the teacher what he had done.

Now lead the following discussion:

- What do you think the teacher did?
- If you were the teacher, what would you do?
- If Joey had come to you at lunch, before he talked to the teacher, what would you have told him to do?
- What did Joey lose by confessing his error? *Probably a lower grade; maybe his parents found out.*
- What did he gain? *Peace of mind that comes from doing the right thing.*

Confession involves risk—you take a chance that admitting your sin to someone will have some painful results. But even those consequences are usually temporary and are far outweighed by the benefits of sharing what you've done.

APPLY

Option 1: Confessing Jesus as Lord. For this option, you need Bibles, masking tape and two chairs.

Ask for a volunteer to read Romans 10:9-10 while junior-highers follow along. Explain that the Bible uses the word "confess" both in reference to confessing sin and to confessing Jesus as Lord. Confessing Jesus as Lord needs to happen only once, and then we can be confident that we are saved. Confessing our sins to each other happens many times through the course of our lives, because it's through confession that God shapes us into the kind of person he wants us to be.

Put a chair in front of your room and tape a large circle around it. Ask for two volunteers, one to represent himself or herself and the other to represent Jesus. Ask the first volunteer (let's call him Hank) to sit on the chair.

Explain that this circle represents Hank's life, and Hank is sitting in the driver's seat of his life. Hank goes to church and hears that Jesus died on the cross and rose from the dead to give him eternal and abundant life. Hank wants to be saved from his sin. So he says . . .

(Let Hank see the book and read the next line to the other volunteer.)

Hank: "Jesus, my driving is a mess and I'm going to get myself killed. I need You to come into my life, save me from myself and my sin, and take control of the wheel of my life."

Then you continue: Jesus steps into Hank's life and sits down at the wheel. (Invite the student playing Jesus to do so. Start to put the second chair next to the first, then move it in front of Hank and have Jesus sit there). Now, Hank doesn't sit in the passenger's seat, like you might think. He is not Jesus' navigator. That's the Holy Spirit's seat. No, Hank sits in the back seat and willingly goes where God takes him. That's what it means to confess Jesus as Lord. Your car (or life) goes where God takes it rather than where you might think it should go. But you gain a vital relationship with God and you don't have to worry about where you're headed.

Hank confessed Jesus as Lord because he recognized that he, a sinner, needed Jesus to save him. From now on, Hank can still confess his sins to God, but he'll also need the support of a community of Christians with whom he can be honest about his ongoing struggles with sins.

Allow the volunteers to be seated and ask someone to read Romans 10:9-10 again while junior-highers follow along. Explain that students can choose right now to believe in Jesus and confess Him as Lord. Allow a moment for silent prayer, then invite students to raise their hand and say aloud "I confess Jesus is Lord" if they feel ready to do so. Thank God for His great gift of salvation and for any who have accepted that gift.

Option 2: Bearing with One Another in Love. For this option, you need paper, pens or pencils, and Bibles.

Read John 8:34 and explain that, just like people become addicted to drugs or alcohol, everyone is addicted to sin. Pass out paper and pens. Pray aloud that the Holy Spirit would convict students of sin, and then ask students to write on their paper any sins that come to mind. Encourage junior-highers to use this time to confess their sins to God.

After a few minutes, assign two volunteers to read James 5:16 and Ephesians 4:2. Explain that the Bible tells us to confess to one another and be humble, to pray for and bear with one another in love. You probably wrote several sins on your paper. You don't have to confess them to us, but if you're willing, we will pray for you and support you.

Ask students to agree that anything said will remain confidential, and be prepared to confess your own sins if needed to get the ball rolling. Ask students to confess by completing this statement: "Hi, I'm John, a recovering sin addict. I (fill in the blank with a sin)."

When everyone who wants to has confessed, lead students in a time of prayer for each other. Close by reading John 8:36 and thanking God for the freedom from sin that Jesus offers. As students leave, have a trashcan available for them to dispose of the paper on which they wrote their sins.

Youth Leader Tip

If you've taught through this book, you can use this option as a review by focusing the confession on sins of friendship. Use the contents page to remind students what they've learned over the last several weeks, and then ask them to confess sins specifically related to those topics.

REFLECT

The following short devotions are for the students to reflect on and answer during the week. You can make a copy of these pages and distribute to your class or print out from the PDF available online at **www.gospellight.com/ uncommon_jh_parents_and_family.zip**.

1—I CONFESS

Don't wait . . . read Psalm 38:18 and take it to heart!

Paula's not supposed to cuss. Not only is she trying to follow Jesus in her words and actions, but cussing is also against her parents' rules.

Today she slipped up. She had auditioned for the school play, and this afternoon when the cast list went up, Paula saw that she didn't make it. The first thing out of her mouth was a four-letter word. No one else heard, but Paula and God both know the truth.

Every night after she climbs into bed, Paula's dad comes in for a few minutes to talk about her day and pray with her. Paula usually looks forward to the time spent with Dad and God, but tonight she's dreading it. When her dad asks about her day, what should Paula say?

- ❏ "It was fine. I didn't make the school play, but I don't care."
- ❏ "I didn't make the school play and I felt really bad about it. Then I made it worse by saying a swear word. I'm sorry."
- ❏ "My day was great! How was yours?"

Is there something you need to confess to a family member or friend? Remember: God already knows the truth, but Christians need to be honest with each other.

2—NOT GUILTY

You'll be glad to know that Romans 10:9 is really good news.

Fill in the blanks below:

If you _____ with your _____, "Jesus is Lord," and _____ in your _____ that God raised him from the dead, _____ _____ ____ _____ (Romans 10:9).

There are times when the weight of sin just doesn't feel lifted, even after we've sought God's forgiveness and confessed to other believers. We continue to feel guilty for mistakes we made in the past and are afraid that maybe we aren't really forgiven.

The apostle Paul must have felt that way sometimes. Before he met Jesus, Paul (who was then called "Saul") treated Christians very badly—he even approved when one of them was stoned to death! (Check out Acts 7:54–8:1 for the full story.) But Paul also knew that his (and our) salvation does not depend on how we are feeling. In his letter to the Christians in Ephesus, he wrote, "It is by grace you have been saved, through faith—and this not from yourselves, it is the gift of God" (Ephesians 2:8). Salvation depends on faith in God's grace, not on feeling okay about ourselves.

Are you feeling guilty about a sin that you have already confessed to God and another Christian? Write a short prayer on the lines below, thanking God for His grace and asking His Spirit to encourage you.

_____

_____

_____

_____

If you're still struggling with guilt, talk with a parent, youth leader or pastor and ask a friend to pray with you.

3—MAKE IT RIGHT

Before you pray, prepare yourself with Mark 11:25.

Bobby was *so* mad at his younger sister. Brit had asked to borrow one of his video games and then lost it! After she had looked everywhere and still could not find it, she came to his room and confessed, promising to save up and replace it. But Brit's allowance is only $10 a week, and that means Bobby won't get a new game for two months—at least!

Bobby was still fuming when he came to church this morning. Now he's sitting in the back, wondering why it's so hard to worship. He usually loves to sing praise songs with his church, but today he can't concentrate. All he can think about is how hateful he was to Brit when she apologized. She tried to do the right thing by confessing, and he threw it back in her face.

Now it's Bobby's turn to confess.

Are you holding a grudge against a family member or friend who hurt you? Why are you waiting to forgive him or her?

_____

_____

_____

_____

In the last part of today's verse, Jesus seems to imply that refusing to forgive others lets our heavenly Father know that we're not serious about having our own sins forgiven. What do you think about this?

_____

_____

_____

_____

4—DAILY CONFESSION

Every day is a good day for confession. Hebrews 3:13 says so!

In some churches, Christians are given an opportunity to confess every day. The pastor, who is known as a *priest* in Catholic and Episcopalian churches, is available to anyone at a certain time each day to hear their confessions and pray with them. Believers in these kinds of churches know that it's a very good idea to keep the slate clean. "I'll deal with my sin tomorrow instead of today" is a lot like saying "I'll take a shower tomorrow instead of today": If you say it for very many days in a row, you end up downright filthy.

You may not belong to a church that offers daily confession, but that does not mean you can't confess daily to a family member or friend! Why not talk to your mom, dad, youth leader, a close Christian friend or your accountability group about spending 5-10 minutes a day talking through your mistakes and how to make them right?

Make a list below of two or three people who might be willing to be your "daily confessor"—and then let them know you can be one, too!

_____

_____

_____

_____

SETTING THE SPIRITUAL TONE IN YOUR FAMILY

If you could start over in youth ministry, what would you do differently?

It's a great question, and one I've been thinking about a lot lately. I've been in youth ministry for more than 22 years, and I just started leading a small group of eleventh grade girls at my church. So I feel like I've got a bit of a new start with these girls—a new chance to build new relationships with new girls.

Here's my answer to that question: If I could start over in youth ministry, I would have talked with God a whole lot more. I'm not talking about my "talks" or my messages; I talked about God plenty then. I'm thinking about in my one-on-one or small-group conversations with kids.

So often I was afraid to bring up God in my conversations with kids. In the name of "relational ministry," I was high on toilet papering, frozen yogurt runs, and overnighters. I was low on honest conversations about how God intersects with my girls' lives—and my own.

When you talk with kids, family issues inevitably emerge. Here are some questions I try to ask kids, especially the girls in my small group:

- What do you think God would say about what you're experiencing with your parents?
- What does it look like to experience Jesus in your home today?
- How can you honor your parents in the midst of what's happening with your family right now?

Part of what motivates me to connect students' family lives with their re-lationship with God is a girl in my group named Alia. Alia's parents were new believers when they brought her to our church. Alia, also a new believer, quickly dove into our youth ministry. She attended every event, loved wel-coming new people, and ended up being one of our ministry's core kids.

Alia ended up setting the spiritual tone in her family. Her parents also grew by leaps and bounds, largely because of the way their own daughter in-spired them.

Granted, Alia's spiritual maturity in her family is the exception, not the norm. But every parent of teenagers knows that their kid often sets the tone for the household. If they're full of sunshine and light, the rest of the family is more likely to be a bit brighter as well. If they're stormy, the rest of the fam-ily is probably grey and cloudy too.

So the next time you're grabbing a drink with a kid, learn from my mistakes and try asking a question that helps them think about how God relates to their home life. They might not be able to connect the dot between God and their family on their own, but a little nudging from you might just do the trick.

Kara Powell
Executive Director of the Fuller Youth Institute
Assistant Professor of Youth, Family and Culture
Fuller Theological Seminary

ENDNOTES

Session 1: Making It Easy
1. When Noah woke up, he cursed Canaan, Ham's son (see Genesis 9:25). This is the first time anyone in the Bible is recorded as uttering a curse. Why did Noah curse Canaan instead of Ham? We don't know for sure, but it might be because God had pronounced His blessing on Noah and Noah's sons (see v. 1), so Noah might have been reluctant to go against what God had just done. Whatever the reason, because Noah repleated the curse three times (see vv. 25-27), it's pretty clear that he meant it.
2. Adapted from Lawrence G. and Andrea J. Enscoe, "Anointed with Oil," *Skit'omatic* (Ventura, CA: Gospel Light, 1993), pp. 49-51.

Session 2: Available Advice
1. Jethro's advice to Moses was totally in line with God's plan for the Israelites at that time. Jethro's words reinforced the role of Moses as mediator between God and humankind. The Israelites' problems were numerous, and Jethro was interested in keeping Moses sane while at the same time making sure that the Israelites were guided by wise and godly leaders.

Session 3: Glued Together or Torn Apart?
1. In Matthew 19:4-9, Jesus was presented with an interesting dilemma. At that time, views of divorce varied from the belief that a man should never divorce his wife to allowing him to just write a letter of divorce and send her on her way. If Jesus took sides on this issue, He would risk offending one or the other groups. Instead, He simply reiterated God's view of marriage: that God had instituted marriage for human blessedness and completeness. God's intention was to make two people one: a oneness that should be difficult to break.
2. "Divorce Counseling May Help Prevent Teen Substance Abuse," U.S. Department of Health and Human Services, 2002. http://family.samhsa.gov/be/counseling.aspx.

Session 4: Closer Than You Think
1. Adapted from Wayne Rice, *More Hot Illustrations for Youth Talks* (Grand Rapids, MI: Zondervan, 1995), pp. 91-92.

Session 5: Who's First?
1. In Jesus' day, it was almost seen as a move of piety to rid oneself of material possessions for God. However, at the same time, Jews were very family-oriented. Their heritage was in their families, and they were fiercely devoted to them. So in Matthew 19:28-30, Jesus is basically saying, "That which you've counted as really important isn't as important as following God."

Session 6: A Second Family
1. The word "devoted" used to describe the Early Church in Acts 2:42 is translated from the Greek *proskartereo*, which literally means "a steadfast and single-minded fidelity to a certain course of action." In other words, these people wouldn't be swayed away from their commitment to loving and living in a community with each other.

Unit 1 Conclusion: How to Resolve Conflicts with Family Members
1. Adapted from Jim Burns, *The Word on Family* (Ventura, CA: Gospel Light, 1997), p. 121.

Session 8: Keeping the Peace
1. Adapted from Doug Fields and Eddie James, *Videos That Teach* (Grand Rapids, MI: Zondervan, 1999). Used by permission.

2. David Jackman, *Mastering the Old Testament, vol. 7: Judges, Ruth* (Dallas, TX: Word, Inc., 1991), pp. 250-251; Lawrence O. Richards, *The Teacher's Commentary* (Wheaton, IL: Victor Books, 1987); *The New Bible Dictionary* (Wheaton, IL: Tyndale House Publishers, Inc., 1962).

Session 9: The Truth, and Nothing But

1. When Peter asked Ananias, "How is it that Satan has so filled your heart" (Acts 5:3), he didn't mean that Ananias was demon-possessed or even that he wasn't a follower of Christ. In fact, the Bible gives no reason to believe that Ananias and Sapphira were not believers. Instead, they had allowed the enemy to get them so worked up over an idea that they got carried away and couldn't see the consequences. It is similar to what happened to Judas prior to betraying Jesus (see Luke 22:3). Since the enemy seeks to devour believers (1 Peter 5:8), we have to especially be on our guard against the "little white lies" that can easily spiral out of control.
2. Adapted from William J. Bennett, *The Book of Virtues* (New York: Simon & Schuster, 1993), pp. 636-637.

Session 10: After You

1. God's blessings on Abram and Lot ironically created a problem: They had too many animals in order to continue to dwell in the same place. They had lived semi-nomadic lives, moving about in partially settled areas in order to find pasture for their flocks. Abram had recently acquired a number of new animals in Egypt, including sheep, cattle, donkeys and camels (Genesis 12:16). Genesis 13:7 mentions that the Canaanites and Perizzites also occupied the area near Bethel, implying that the land was crowded and unable to sustain all of the animals. The Old Testament records similar problems between Isaac and the Philistines (see Genesis 26:12-22), Jacob and Laban (see Genesis 30:43) and Jacob and Esau (see Genesis 36:6-7).
2. Adapted from Doug Fields and Eddie James, *Videos That Teach* (Grand Rapids, MI: Zondervan, 1999). Used by permission.
3. Adapted from William J. Bennett, *The Book of Virtues* (New York: Simon and Schuster, 1993), pp. 271-272.

Session 11: Can We Talk?

1. Adapted from Dennis R. McLaughlin, ed., *The Gigantic Book of Games for Youth Ministry, vol. 1* (Loveland, CO: Group Publishing, Inc., 1999), pp. 269-270.

Session 12: I Confess

1. Adapted from Debbie Gowensmith, ed., *The Gigantic Book of Games for Youth Ministry, vol. 2* (Loveland, CO: Group Publishing, Inc., 1999), pp. 116-117.
2. Ibid., pp. 200-201.
3. James 5:16 clearly teaches that sickness caused by sin can be cured through confession and prayer. However, while God can use sickness for His purpose, we should be slow to assume that sickness has been caused by sin (see the disciples' assumption to that regard and Jesus' response in John 9:1-5).